Beautiful Beaufort by the Sea™ Guidebook

Fifth edition

Current Titles in our
American Coastal Guidebook Series

■ **Beautiful Beaufort by the Sea**tm **Guidebook,** the definitive guidebook to this beloved historic waterfront town in the South Carolina sea islands, now in its fifth edition, illustrated with photographs and historical drawings.

■ **Nantucket Island Guidebook**, continues the tradition of excellence in coastal guidebooks in this fresh look at the far away island of Nantucket, Massachusetts.

■ **Hilton Head Island Guidebook**, covers everything you need to know about this popular resort island on the South Carolina coast.

Beautiful Beaufort by the Sea™ Guidebook

Fifth edition

George Graham Trask, editor

Coastal Villages Press
Beaufort, South Carolina

Tabby Manse

Published by Coastal Villages Press,
a division of Coastal Villages, Inc.,
2614 Boundary Street, Beaufort, SC 29906
843-524-0075 fax 843-525-0000
email: info@coastal-villages.com

Visit our web site: www.coastal-villages.com

Available at special discounts for bulk purchases
and sales promotions from the publisher
and your local bookseller
2 4 6 8 10 9 7 5 3 1

ISBN 1-882943-10-4
Library of Congress Catalog Number: 2001116511

Fifth Edition
Printed in the United States of America

In celebration of the lives of

John Maurice Trask
and
Flora Graham Trask

To see their Beaufort,
look about you

Washington, DC

VA

Lexington

KY

Richmond

Raleigh/Durham

TN   Asheville

Charlotte   NC

Memphis

Greenville   SC

Wilmington

Atlanta

Columbia

MS   AL

Macon

Charleston

Beaufort

Jackson   Greensboro

GA

Savannah

Seaside

Jacksonville

FL

Orlando

Miami

George Trask

Contents

Beautiful Beaufort is enjoyed by residents and visitors alike as they stroll along the Bay at the waterfront park.

Preface and Acknowledgements

This guidebook is a song to that which is unique to a small place on the coast of South Carolina. We have tried to capture the melody of this place, Beaufort and its Sea Island surroundings, and play it in a key that will resonate through the years. The lyrics are history and, perhaps, a tendency to speak adoringly of those things that are especially meaningful to us. Thus we are somewhat heavy on history and a bit boastful about the peculiarities of what is affectionately known as beautiful Beaufort by the sea.

"Beautiful Beaufort by the sea, 26 miles from Yemassee" is a ditty, recited in childhood by people who have grown up here and by U.S. Marine recruits as they get off the train on their way to Parris Island. Yemassee is a tiny town on the mainland in the northernmost corner of Beaufort county, the place where the train stops on its way from New York to Miami.

But Beaufort is not a railroad town, and as we look at this ancient place we are reminded that those who came before us—by the sea—made Beaufort what it is. The sea brought the first inhabitants here, pre-historic American Indians who annually wintered here when cold weather inland pushed them to the warm shores of these Sea Islands. The sea brought the first European explorers here, Spaniards in tiny sailing vessels across a treacherous ocean almost 500 years ago. The sea brought the first settlers here, Frenchmen, Scotsmen, and Englishmen, the latter establishing the town of Beaufort in 1711. The sea brought the aristocratic planters here, lured by rich soil and mild weather. The sea brought the African laborers here, toiling on the indigo, rice, and cotton plantations until released from slavery by an invading army. And the sea brought the in-

vading army here, the cataclysm in 1861 that changed everything.

Living in Beaufort at any time from the beginning of the
Civil War until the end of the 20th century, a period of almost
150 years, has carried a peculiar charm. One discovered early a
special quality about the place. It wasn't typically Southern.
There were all those permanent residents whose parents and
grandparents hailed from Massachusetts and New York and
Pennsylvania. It was only after taking a closer look that one un-
derstood: Beaufort was both Southern and Northern.

Until November 1861 Beaufort was entirely Southern, in-
habited by some of the richest people on the North American
continent, a planter aristocracy, and by their minions on cotton
and rice plantations, 10,000 slaves. Then in one of those dis-
continuous, cataclysmic events that mark the absolute end of an
age and the beginning of another, the white Southerners disappeared, run off in one day by an invading force of 30,000 Yankees. Remember now, this was in 1861 at the beginning of the
Civil War, only six months after the fall of Fort Sumter.

Replacing the white Southerners were a horde of Northern
soldiers, a handful of Northern idealists, assorted land speculators, and 10,000 abandoned slaves. After the war the soldiers
and the speculators departed. The idealists as school teachers,
farmers, and merchants, and the former slaves as freedmen
owning 40 acres and a mule, remained. Slowly, a few white
Southerners returned, not the aristocrats run off by the Yankees, but working-class people. All thrown together in the af-
termath of war, these disparate cultural and racial groups were
forced by circumstance to learn how to live and work together,
a blending of South and North in this old seacoast Southern
town.

Thus Beaufort became in the 20th century a place different
from the Old South, lacking the typical memories of the War
Between the States, as many white Southerners in other parts of

the South still called the unpleasantness. Lacking also the destruction of the war, epitomized by William Tecumseh Sherman, the man who brought fire, rape, and poverty to South Carolina but friendship and hope to Beaufort. For, you see, Sherman's closest friends and fellow soldiers from his West Point days were living in luxury in Beaufort when he marched from Atlanta to the sea, and from the sea to Columbia, which he burned to the ground. Sherman had no reason to burn Beaufort. On the contrary, he celebrated Beaufort as Northern ground, not Southern, and came here by boat from Savannah to visit his friends immediately before his army's invasion of South Carolina in early 1865.

Perhaps this unexpected amalgam of cultures, wrought by war, was why Northerners seemed so much at home in Beaufort but why Southerners, both black and white, continued to impress their enduring history and values on this place. But the Beaufort of old is changing. The roads into town are becoming less picturesque as traffic increases and the asphalt is widened. The rural land is becoming less open as residential subdivisions and strip shopping areas replace forests and fields.

Formerly placid vistas at night over broad expanses of darkened water are now lit on the distant shores with floodlights and flashing radio and cellular telephone towers. Newcomers proclaim their desire to keep Beaufort from changing, yet their arrival causes the change. We must all be careful not to destroy what is unique here.

Many people have contributed the ideas, written the words, and, above all, provided the encouragement for this book, now in its fifth edition. Encouragement is the key ingredient, for producing a book by a small-press publisher is today, at its core, a sole and a lonely activity. In the past the talents of scores of people working for a number of companies might have been required. Due to the economics of the small-press industry today and to the technology of the computer, all of these people have been replaced in most respects by one person. Of all the tasks, only the printing and the binding are done commercially.

Among the many persons who have contributed so much to the success of this book over the years, special thanks go to:

Marie Bernice La Touche Wilson, who wrote the first words that evolved into this book. A native of La Jolla, California, and a graduate with a degree in rhetoric from the University of California at Berkeley, Marie first saw the need to provide visitors to Beaufort with accurate local information. With zeal, perseverance, a happy way with words, and a diversity of technical skills, she did the many jobs necessary in collaboration with the undersigned—both of us erstwhile editors-in-chief of our high-school newspapers—to produce the first two editions. Marie continues to pursue her creativity in an area of Florida not unlike the Beaufort of today.

Rebecca Kaufmann Crowley from the university town of Durham, New Hampshire. A Swarthmore graduate, a superb researcher and writer, a skillful certified public accountant, and a mother of two children. Becky came to Beaufort all the way from the Peace Corps in Botswana to help write and revise books, including the third edition. Becky keeps in touch with Beaufort these days by e-mail from Texas.

Janet Carr Hull, Beaufort native, whose enthusiasm for her home town has been exceeded only by her helping hand with the fourth edition and by her friendship to many of the people recognized here. To Janet is owed special gratitude for her ability to simplify convoluted paragraphs from the early editions and for her contributions to the chapter on Beaufort's cinematic scene.

Shannon McLaughlin Dupree, the most versatile person in the world. Shannon is the only human being alive who managed to earn a degree with a perfect 4.0 average from the University of Maryland while stationed in Okinawa with her

Marine-aviator husband, simultaneously rearing five children. Shannon and Frank now live in Phoenix, Arizona.

Lisa Kassuba Hudson, general manager extraordinaire of Sea Island Inn in historic downtown Beaufort. Lisa has made more recommendations to visitors about where to enjoy a good evening meal in downtown Beaufort than anyone can reckon.

Betty K. Cunningham, the dry wit who espied the first and still the only grammatical error found in any of the first three editions. For that happy discovery she was given the pleasure of helping to proofread the fourth edition. Errors thereafter are solely due to the ignorance and laziness of the undersigned.

Chris Stanley and Will Balk of Bay Street Trading Company, cheerful bibliophiles, whose brains have been picked a thousand times to learn what people want to read about Beaufort.

Dr. Lawrence Rowland, a Beaufort native, a lifelong friend, and a professor of history at the University of South Carolina at Beaufort. Larry contributed for the first edition his excellent brief history of the Beaufort area, covering a period of almost 500 years.

Robert E. Cuttino, a graduate of Yale Divinity School and the beloved retired pastor of The Baptist Church of Beaufort. Bob continues to help keep alive the memory of that greatest of Beaufortonians, Richard Fuller, a son of Harvard.

Gerhard Spieler, whose weekly essays for more than 20 years in *The Beaufort Gazette* have helped fill the blanks in the scope of Beaufort's lengthy history.

Roger Pinckney, age 91, a master builder of Lowcountry docks and a colorful member of the venerable Pinckney family of South Carolina. Roger knows first-hand the entire history of Beaufort, having lived almost a century of it himself.

G.G. Dowling, resident of Bay Street, dean of the Beaufort bar, and an admiring friend who always casts a write-in vote for the undersigned for President. G.G. carries in his head more knowledge about Beaufort since the Civil War than can be gleaned from all the books in the library.

Penelope Rhoads Chitty, literary critic, dear and sorely missed friend, and beautiful lady of the first rank, whose clear eyes for a hard fact and a good phrase were sharpened at Swarthmore College and the Central Intelligence Agency. Penny closed her eyes forever early on the fair, quiet, beautiful Beaufort morning of May 28, 1997. Her serene monument stands in the graveyard of St. Helena's Episcopal Church.

My wonderful wife, Constance Claire Bowen Trask, and our three wonderful children, Graham Bowen Trask, Christian Whitmire Trask, and Claire Everlee Trask, who are my truest critics, my greatest supporters, and my best friends.

My mother, Flora Graham Trask, age 88 and still going strong, who first urged that this book be published and who holds the record for having purchased more copies of it than any other person on earth. She is the best mother in the world to me and my three brothers, and she is the apple of our eyes.

My father, John Maurice Trask, to me the greatest man in the world, who did not live to see this book in any of its incarnations, but who, together with my mother, left an indelible mark on their four sons and on Beaufort. I and the people of Beaufort owe to them a debt of gratitude that can never be repaid.

While Beaufort has grown a good bit recently, it still hasn't grown 400% the way this book has since its first edition—proof that there is still no way one can say enough good things about beautiful Beaufort by the sea.

George Graham Trask
February 15, 2001

My Favorite Town

The spell was cast as we turned off the main route, pursuing the vague report of an old and quiet city out among
the sea islands. The approach to Beaufort threads through
broad marshlands and across shining rivers. There are far
vistas of wooded islets, unpeopled and unapproachable
across the high-waving reeds of the morasses. The effect
is strangely other-worldly. One's initial response to a lo-
cality is likely to be made up of trivialities. There was a
feeling of unreality in the spectacle of five dollars' worth
of terrapin on the hoof, leisurely crossing the highway
and vanishing in the tawny depths of the marsh where
two snowy egrets posed in philosophic reverie. It set a
keynote. We entered the town proper between a long
double row of royal palmettos and rounded a curve to
blink amazedly at a floral riot in a privet yard. There were
camellias enough in that one clump to choke the biggest
display window on Fifth Avenue. Overhead a pair of
chinaberry trees were festooned with the soft gray of the
Spanish moss and spangled with the golden traceries of
the wild jasmine. For background there spread the broad
expanse of reed and river with a lordly white yacht on its
way to Florida, poised in mid-stream while two sweating
bridge-tenders toiled at the hand-lever of the turntable,
aided by a pair of sails which they had rigged on the ironwork.

We turned to one another. "This is it," we said.

—Samuel Hopkins Adams, © 1950 Ford Motor Co.

George Trask

Palmettos, the South Carolina state tree, stand like soldiers at attention in front of Beaufort's arsenal, now the city's museum.

Basic Facts about Beaufort

■ Beaufort county is the 12th largest of the 46 counties in South Carolina. It is the fastest growing county in the state.

	Population	Increase
2000 (estimated)	110,000	27%
1990	86,425	32%
1980	65,364	28%
1970	51,136	15%
1960	44,187	64%
1950	26,993	22%
1940	22,037	

■ The City of Beaufort is the county seat and, though growing fast and called a city, is still a small town.

2000 (estimated)	12,000	25%
1990	9,576	9%
1980	8,634	

■ Beaufort lies in the subtropical climate zone, enjoying four distinct seasons but without extremes of heat or cold. Gardening, golf, and other outdoor activities are enjoyed twelve months a year. Fall arrives late and spring arrives early.

Average temperature:	January 49.2°	July 81.2°
Mean temperature:	Low 55.1°	High 76.7°
Earliest freeze date	November 11	
Latest freeze date	March 11	
Mean yearly precipitation	50 inches	
Average midday humidity	53 percent	

■ Beaufort is located off the beaten track. No interstate high-ways traverse the county and you don't drive through Beaufort on a trip anywhere except to the beach. Beaufort is a destination in itself, but is easy to reach by water, land, and air.

Nearest navigable waterway	Out your front door
Nearest oceanfront beach	Hunting Island, 12 miles
Nearest interstate highway	I-95, 25 miles
Nearest world-famous resort	Hilton Head Island, 30 miles
Nearest major airports:	Savannah, GA, 45 miles
	Charleston, SC, 65 miles
Nearest megacity	Atlanta, GA, 270 miles
Nearest chaos	Washington DC, 540 miles

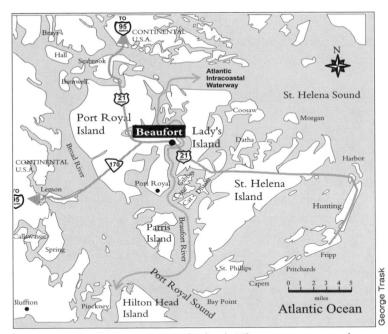

Beaufort is located on Port Royal Island. There is more water than land in the area, and almost as much marshland as high ground.

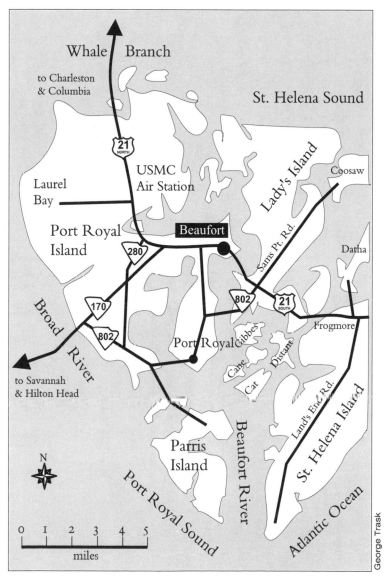

There are only two ways to drive to the mainland, north over the
Whale Branch bridge or west over the Broad River bridge.

George Trask

Hand-wrought ornamental iron work and marble steps of Secession House, c. 1813, signify the wealth of Beaufort before the Civil War.

Beaufort Superlatives

■ Beaufort is located on an island called Port Royal Island. All of the surrounding area—Lady's Island, St. Helena Island, Fripp Island, Hunting Island, Datha Island, Distant Island, Cat Island, Cane Island, Gibbes Island, Parris Island, Spring Island, Callawassie Island, Hilton Head Island, Daufuskie Island, and others comprising scores of islands—make up what are called the South Carolina Sea Islands.

■ Beaufort is far enough north to enjoy four distinct seasons and far enough south to escape bitter winter weather. As a result the growing season here is twelve months. The sandy soil is so rich that all you must do to get something growing is put it in the ground.

■ The normal tidal variation here between low and high tide is eight feet, reaching above eleven feet on "spring tides," one of the greatest variations along the Atlantic coast. Hundreds of thousands of acres of marshland and oyster beds are flooded and exposed twice daily, creating an ever-changing scene of beauty and tranquillity.

■ Until modern-day bridges were constructed, Beaufort and the surrounding islands were reachable only by boat. The first bridge to Lady's Island was not built until the 1920s and the bridge across Broad River toward Hilton Head Island and Savannah not until the late 1950s.

■ Beaufort was the site in 1514 of the second landing by Europeans on the North American continent. The first was Ponce De Leon's landing at St. Augustine, Florida, one year earlier.

■ Beaufort was the site in 1562 of the first Protestant settlement in North America, Jean Ribaut's French Huguenot settlement called Charlesfort.

■ Beaufort, second oldest town in South Carolina and among the oldest in the United States, was chartered in 1711 as Beaufort Town. The only town in South Carolina established earlier is Charleston (known then as Charles Town), chartered in 1670.

■ Before the Civil War (1861-1865), Beaufort was one of the wealthiest towns in the United States and was commonly regarded as the "Newport of the South" by wealthy planters who built grand summer homes here. The South was the richest part of the nation before the Civil War, and some of the richest of the rich lived in Beaufort.

■ With perhaps more antebellum homes per block than any other American town, Beaufort is one of only a handful of places with its entire 304-acre original town designated a National Historic Landmark District.

■ In 1860 the first draft of the Ordinance of Secession of South Carolina from the Union was drawn up in a Beaufort house on Craven Street, now known as Secession House.

■ In 1861, before any of the great Civil War battles, Beaufort was invaded by a great U.S. naval armada and occupied by Federal troops. The invasion was the largest in U.S. Navy history until the 1944 Normandy invasion.

■ Beaufort was occupied by Union army troops throughout the Civil War. Because the town served as Union army headquarters and a Union hospital zone during the war, Beaufort was virtually untouched by the battles, the burning, and the destruction that many other Southern towns experienced.

■ Robert Smalls, a native of Beaufort, captured the imagination of the Union in 1862 by stealing the *Planter*, a Confederate gun-boat. An instant hero, he became after the Civil War one of the first black men to serve in the United States Congress.

■ The Emancipation Proclamation, freeing slaves in areas occupied by Federal troops during the Civil War, was first applied on January 1, 1863, to the only major occupied area: Beaufort and the surrounding Sea Islands.

Harper's Weekly, June 14, 1862

Robert Smalls, Beaufort native and hero of the Union, at the time of his famous capture of the Confederate gun-boat Planter *in 1862.*

■ During the Civil War, Penn Normal School on St. Helena Island was founded by Quaker missionaries from Philadelphia as the first school for freed slaves in the United States. Today, it remains a center of black culture, known as Penn Center. In the early 1960s, Dr. Martin Luther King, Jr., and his staff planned his famous March On Washington at retreats on the Penn campus.

■ Newly-freed slaves in the Beaufort area were given the opportunity during the Civil War to purchase 40 acres and a mule for a nominal sum from the Federal government, the origin of black land ownership in the South and a major reason for the stability of Gullah culture on the Sea Islands.

■ After the Civil War, Beaufort's economy was supported first by phosphate mining and then by large-scale truck farming. Thousands of acres produced fresh green vegetables, shipped nationwide. The soil here is some of the richest in the world and the climate affords a year-round growing season.

■ Military bases have existed at Beaufort since the Civil War, growing into one of the area's most important industries. Three military installations call Beaufort home: Marine Corps Recruit Depot Parris Island, Marine Corps Air Station Beaufort, and U.S. Naval Hospital Beaufort.

■ In the 1950s, tourism growth began with resort development on Hilton Head and Fripp Islands, both located in Beaufort county. Numerous other islands in the county have since been developed, giving the entire area a vigorous tourism and resort industry.

■ In recent years Beaufort has been the picturesque setting of major motion pictures, including *Conrack, The Great Santini,*

The Big Chill, The Prince of Tides, Forrest Gump, The War, Rudyard Kipling's The Jungle Book, Something To Talk About, White Squall, Last Dance, G.I. Jane, Forces of Nature, and *Rules of Engagement.*

■ Travel articles and photographs of Beaufort's historic homes and scenic waterways appear almost weekly in newspapers and magazines nationwide. A full-color front page of *The New York Times* Sunday *Travel* section devoted to Beaufort drew worldwide attention. A single issue of *The Sophisticated Traveler* section of *The New York Times* enthusiastically heralded London, Paris, Hong Kong and...Beaufort. *Vogue* magazine touted Beaufort as "the South's hottest small town," and *Vogue* wasn't referring to the temperature.

■ Beaufort is one of the "Top Ten Places To Live" according to *Outside* magazine. Beaufort ranks 23d among the "100 Best Small Towns in America" according to *Newsweek* magazine and is one of the "100 Top Art Towns in America" according to a recent book of that name. *Fortune* has magazine dubbed Beaufort as "Shangri-La" and *Coastal Living* magazine has proclaimed it as "reminiscent of early Carmel and Nantucket, a hip place about to happen."

These superlatives remind us of the many ways that Beaufort is a special place. The challenge for Beaufortonians is to keep it a special place as it grows into a larger place.

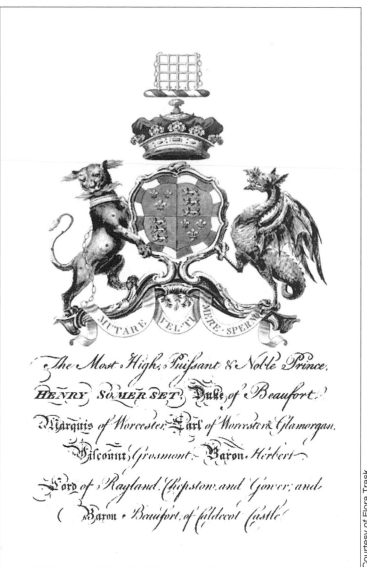

Coat of arms of Henry Somerset, Duke of Beaufort, for whom the town of Beaufort was named by the Lords Proprietor in 1711.

Special Beaufort Words

■ **Beaufort**. The town is named after Henry Somerset (1684-1714). the second Duke of Beaufort, who in 1709 became one of the Lords Proprietor, owners of all of Carolina under a grant from the British Crown. In 1711 at Somerset's home, Beaufort Castle, the Proprietors decided upon a new town in Carolina south of Charleston named Beaufort.

The pronunciation has been the source of much confusion. The word looks like it should be pronounced the French way, BO-FOR (rhymes with "go for"), or the North Carolina way, BO-FOOT (rhymes with "no foot"). Here we say BEW-FOOT (starts like the first syllable in "beautiful").

On a recent trip to Beaufort, North Carolina, the current Duke of Beaufort was asked by a charming young woman why South Carolinians pronounce the name of their town unconventionally, to which he replied, "My dear, because South Carolinians don't know how to talk."

Others have suggested that our pronunciation, like our town, is linked visually and aurally to the word "beautiful," which would tend to fuel embers of subtle rivalry between North and South Carolina. During the 18th century, North Carolina was commonly known as "poor Carolina" and South Carolina as "rich Carolina." North Carolina is still known by some as "the valley of humility between two mountains of conceit," referring to its neighboring states, South Carolina and Virginia.

The practical answer is that our pronunciation differs to distinguish our town in the minds of people who don't otherwise know the difference. More subjectively, we know it is both different from any other place and undeniably beautiful, attracting our focus to this tribute to our town, beautiful Beaufort by the sea in South Carolina.

■ **Beaufort Bay**. This deep, wide, protected portion of the Beaufort River, facing south toward the ocean and over which the high bluff of Bay Street looks, is the reason why the town is situated here. Residential mansions and shops line the waterfront. In the distance is Parris Island. The Bay contains a large sand bar where funloving power boaters anchor at low tide, setting up volleyball nets for summer frolic until the rising tide drives them away. Sailboaters enjoy the Bay all year long.

Steamer Cliveden *of the Beaufort & Savannah Line carried people to and from the mainland in early 1900s before the bridges were built.*

■ **Beaufort River**. Technically not a river, this large body of tidal water, part of the Atlantic Intracoastal Waterway, runs from Port Royal Sound in the direction of Savannah up past the town of Beaufort to St. Helena Sound in the direction of Charleston. Before bridges connected these islands to the mainland, steamers ran in the Beaufort River carrying people and supplies to and from Savannah and Charleston. Tides run rapidly, with the normal variation from low to high tide being an extraordinary eight feet. Although the marked channel is very deep, there are sandbars scattered about. Wise boaters read the coastal charts, especially at low tide.

■ **Beaufort Salute**. The film crew for *The Great Santini* coined the term "Beaufort salute," referring to the method of flicking your hand over your face to shoo away the "no see ums," which are sand gnats that swarm over Lowcountry baseball games, picnics, and Parris Island recruit trainees.

■ **Beaufort Style**. Now that Beaufort has become chic, the old homes have suddenly acquired in the eyes of architectural sophisticates their own "style," described at some length elsewhere in this book. Beaufort's mansions overlooking the water, with wide porches, raised basements, and classical porticos, have always been distinctive. If you are constructing a house in the "Beaufort style" here, remember that the front of your house should face south, no matter where the street is. Style has other meanings in Beaufort, too. When you call the plumber because your sink is stopped up and she arrives three days later because she went fishing instead of hastening to you, she is "arriving in the Beaufort style." When your city friends are running themselves ragged in life's rat race and you are happy as a clam on a mud bank down here in Beaufort, you are "living in the Beaufort style."

■ **Dove Shoot**. One of God's greatest glories are mourning doves, small, pigeon-like, migratory gray birds with whistling in their wings when they fly. In springtime they come here to mate on their way northward. Fall brings them back south, stopping off here for a rest, snacking on native seeds in woods and fields before proceeding to Mexico. For centuries Southern boys have lurked at field's edge with shotgun ready, hoping to fell one of these morsels to take home to mamma for supper. The doves have the advantage. In spring, when the law prevents shooting them, they are as friendly as your neighborhood squirrel. In autumn, when the sun gets low in the sky and you've been waiting in the field all afternoon, they dart out at 200 miles an hour, turning sideways flips just as you raise your trusty sixteen-gauge skyward, blinded by the sun's glare. Good old boys and girls, and Yankees too, often come home empty handed; politically-correct spoilsports refuse to understand.

George Trask

Shooting skeet (clay targets) is the lazy man's way of going to a dove shoot in Beaufort, quicker and cheaper, but not nearly so much fun.

■ **Frogmore**. Frogmore is best described as a state of mind. Locals also know it as a reference to a crossroads along Highway 21 on St. Helena Island. The crossroads was linked to a nearby cotton plantation named for a royal palace in England. Improbably, the name stuck to the crossroads. Some folks here have tried fervently to get rid of "Frogmore," but it keeps coming back, just like frogs do.

■ **Frogmore International Airport**. A tongue-in-cheek reference, coined by colorful local radio personality and raconteur Bill Peters, to our illustrious county airport on Lady's Island, up the road from that croaking crossroads called Frogmore that we told you about a minute ago. You can trust that no international flights land here. In fact, there is no commercial service at all at this airport. You may purchase T-shirts

George Trask

with "Frogmore International" printed on them here. Lady's Island Airport is the official name.

■ **Frogmore Stew**. The world's simplest gourmet feast, this tasty combination of shrimp, sausage, corn on the cob, onions, and bay spice is a local tradition. The name hails from Frogmore on St. Helena Island, presumably where the dish originated. Here's the recipe for Frogmore's gift to mankind:

Frogmore Stew

Serves approximately 10. Add more of everything to the water and seasoning if your guests haven't eaten in a week:

2 gallons water approximately
4 tablespoons Old Bay Seasoning or equivalent
1 medium onion chopped
2 pounds smoked sausage cut into 2-inch lengths
5 ears corn halved
3 pounds shrimp

Bring water to a boil in a large pot and add seasoning, onion, and sausage. Return to boil. Add corn and return to boil until done, about 15 minutes. Add shrimp, stirring often, until they turn just pink, about 4 minutes. Do not overcook the shrimp. Drain and serve with butter or cocktail sauce on table covered with newspaper for easy cleanup. Eat with your fingers and use paper towels like people in Frogmore do. Mmmmmmmm, good!

■ **Gullah**. A pride of African-American culture is Gullah, a term describing a geographical area centered on the Sea Islands surrounding Beaufort; cultural characteristics of the black people living on these islands; and their particular dialect bordering on a separate language. The Gullah dialect has long been recognized and appreciated for its richness and colorfulness. A studious translation of the Bible into Gullah testifies to its enduring qualities. Recent scholarship indicates that the ancestors of today's Gullah originated in Sierra Leone on Africa's west coast. Brought here as slaves in the 18th century, they gained freedom in the earliest days of the Civil War due to the Federal invasion here in 1861. Many descendants remained on these islands, carrying forward strong culture and pride. Art, literature, and scholarly works by and about Gullah people bring keen appreciation of their unique place in the American mosaic. The springtime Gullah Festival on downtown Beaufort's waterfront now attracts thousands of visitors to Beaufort.

A Gullah Tale

Oncet Ber Rabbit an' Ber Wolf buy a cow togeder. Den Ber Rabbit kill de cow, an' Ber Wolf didn' know it. Ber Rabbit take de cow tail an' stick un down in de dirt an' run, gone ter call de wolf. An' tell de wolf, "Le' um pull on de cow tail, see ef he could get de cow up!" Den, when dey pull, de cow tail come off. Said, "Cow gone down in de groun'." After Ber Wolf gone, Ber Rabbit gone to get de meat to kyarry home for his fader.

—Elsie Clews Parsons, *Folk-Lore of the Sea Islands, South Carolina,* ©1923 American Folk-Lore Society

■ **Hurricanes**. These occasional visitors to Beaufort have in recent decades borne such names as Gracie, David, Hugo, and Fran. One of the measures of a hurricane's force is its wind speed, measured by what is called, appropriately enough, the Beaufort scale. In 1806, Sir Francis Beaufort, a British admiral, developed a scale from 1 to 12 to be used to estimate the force of wind, with calm being 0 and 12 being hurricane force. Beaufortonians pay close attention to the Beaufort scale. Hurricane paths are as unpredictable as life itself. They have been known to dip southerly, and even to loop inland and push back out to sea to threaten new areas on their destructive missions. Wise Beaufortonians skip the hurricane party, tune in the Weather Channel, and evacuate to the mainland when told to do so by the authorities.

Residents inspect hurricane damage from safety of their automobiles after 1940 storm, the storm of the century to Beaufort old-timers.

■ **Live Oak**. Live oak (*Quercus virginiana*), one of the finest of the many varieties of oaks in the world, ranks among Beaufortonians as a national treasure. An evergreen, it sheds its leaves in early spring just as a new crop of leaves appears. Trunks can reach almost 12 feet in diameter with limbs spreading three times as far as the towering height. The U.S. Navy's early sailing fleet was built almost entirely of live oak, the *USS Constitution*, known as "Old Ironsides," being the most famous vessel. The keel of "Old Ironsides" still includes a 150-foot length of live oak, installed when the warship was built in 1797. When Hurricane Hugo came through South Carolina in September 1989 it uprooted many huge, old live oak trees, evidence of the incredible power of that storm. Beaufortonians have passed stringent laws to protect live oaks from being cut down.

Live oak avenue at Beaufort's National Cemetery provides a serene and stately canopy for thousands of Civil War graves.

■ **Lowcountry**. Geologically, the state of South Carolina is divided into three regions, each with distinct terrain, climate, and flora. The Piedmont is the upper part of the state at the foothills of the Appalachian mountains. The Midlands are the middle part of the state with rolling sandy hills. And the Lowcountry is the lower part of the state subject to the influence of the tidal ocean. Part of the Lowcountry is a series of islands, located primarily in Beaufort county, called the Sea Islands. When God made the Lowcountry, especially that part of it known as the Sea Islands, he called it paradise.

Springtime in Beaufort

When jasmines, through the woods, to early spring,
In golden cups, their dewy incense bring,
White dog-wood blossoms sparkle through the trees,
The fragrant grape perfumes the morning breeze,
And with the warmer sun and balmier air,
The finny myriads to their haunts repair;
Such sports are his—with boundless jest and glee,
Where bold Port Royal spreads its mimic sea;
Bright in the North—the length'ning bay and sky
Blent into one—its shining waters lie,
And southward breaking on the shelving shore,
Meet the sea wave and swell its endless roar,
On either hand gay groups of islands show
Their charms reflected in the stream below—
No richer fields, no lovelier isles than these,
No happier homes, the weary traveller sees!

—William J. Grayson, Beaufort, S.C., 1854

■ **Marsh**. The verdant tidal pasture dividing the sea from the islands in our paradise is called marsh, birthplace of much sea life and bird life in this pristine part of our planet. Much of the eastern coastline was covered in marsh in past times, but the folly of man in more industrialized states northward caused much of its destruction. We have always been a gentler sort here in the southland, closer to nature. No one dare destroy marsh here. And no one dare call it swamp.

At a first glance, the marsh may not appear exciting. The more one lives with the ever-changing marsh, the more one falls in love with it. Varying with the tides and the seasons, the marsh is never a still-life picture. Whether the tide is coming in or going out, or the color of the grass is transforming from green to gold, the marsh is always in flux. Have a picnic or spend a lifetime here, you'll see what we mean about the marsh.

Marsh interspersed with tidal creeks characterizes the Sea Islands. For oystermen the marsh provides a livelihood.

George Trask

Beaufortonians enjoy an oyster roast on the high bluff of an island re-treat near downtown Beaufort on a balmy autumn afternoon.

■ **Oyster Roast**. Growing in the fertile tidal mud banks along the marsh is a succulent marine bivalve mollusk known as the oyster. For thousands of years, long before folks arrived here from across the ocean, the native Indians engaged in a peculiar ritual. They waded into the creek, reached down into the mud, pulled up the oyster, washed their shells in the cleansing salt water, spread them over a bed of hot coals with a moist covering at the river bank, then talked and laughed for about ten minutes. The result was roasted oysters, one of life's greatest culinary pleasures. Beaufort sophisticates today do exactly the same as the Indians, but usually arrive for the party in Weejuns and Madras and get somebody else to waddle around in the mud ahead of time. We moderns bettered the Indians in one respect only: cool beer or white wine with which to wash down these delights. Cognoscenti bring their own gloves and oyster knives.

■ **Palmetto Tree**. Because of its name, some folks get the impression that this tree (*Sabal palmetto*) is not a true palm tree. Actually it is a palm tree through and through, growing as high as 60 feet and living as long as 75 years, but not producing coconuts the way its tropical relatives do. See them in formation along the causeway at the Marine Corps Recruit Depot Parris Island and along Beaufort's entrance thoroughfare, Boundary Street. Do not confuse these trees with saw palmetto (*Serenoa repens*), a low shrub with thin, long fronds similar to palmetto leaves. Saw palmetto is also often confused with another local favorite, the yucca plant (*Yucca aloifolia*). The yucca with its chaste white bloom is sometimes called "Spanish bayonet" because of very sharp, pointed leaves. Truth to tell, when you start talking about palmetto trees you get into a complicated subject.

■ **Sea Islands**. All of Beaufort county except a portion on the mainland is composed of hundreds of islands. Flying over in an airplane, you see water everywhere, interspersed with what appear to be sparkling jewels. The jewels are the islands. The sparkle is the water splashing against the marsh grass. This area has been called the Sea Islands since Europeans first set foot here almost five centuries ago. Isolated from the mainland far longer than almost any other area, many of these islands had no bridges until the mid-20th century. Most do not directly face the ocean, but are on nearby tidal rivers, creeks, and bays running to the ocean.

■ **Sea Island Rice and Sea Island Cotton.** The Sea Islands are forever linked with two of the most famous and valuable agricultural crops in history: Sea Island rice and Sea Island cotton. The soil here is a dark, rich, well-drained, sandy loam, the finest soil to grow crops. For centuries farm-

Frank Leslie's Illustrated Newspaper, Feb. 15, 1862

Sea Island cotton being baled on a Beaufort plantation in 1862, the last crop planted by slaves and the first crop harvested by freedmen.

ers have tilled the Sea Islands on plantations of thousands of acres. The employment and wealth created on the Sea Islands, until the rise of the military bases and the resort and retirement communities during the past 40 years, came almost entirely from these lands.

■ **Spanish Moss.** That tangled, curly net draping from our live oaks (and other trees) is not just an ornamental conjuring up memories of the romantic Old South. People use it as upholstery stuffing, and birds love to make their nests with it. Contrary to popular belief, this plant is not Spanish, is not a moss, and does not hurt its host. It is an air plant that lacks interest in soil and so chooses to dangle freely from limbs to catch sunlight and rainwater. Botanically, Spanish moss (*Tillandsia usneoides*) is a member of the pineapple family. If you decide to take some home with you, be sure to put it in a tightly-sealed plastic bag. Heat the moss in your oven or microwave to kill the little red bugs, also known as "chiggers" (another subject entirely). Otherwise, you'll be scratching.

■ **Tabby.** As the Indians feasted on oysters on the sand banks of their island paradise for eons, they tossed the spent oyster shells into big mounds. When the Europeans arrived, accustomed as they were to brick houses, they sought but found no clay here. They invented tabby as a substitute. They dug the ancient oyster shells out of the Indian mounds, burned them over a big fire until they turned into powdered lime, stirred in whole oyster shells, sand, and water, then poured this aggregate into wooden forms to create huge solid walls of tabby, a building material unique to this area. Steadfast and sturdy, tabby houses here have withstood hundreds of years of hurricanes and other violent storms with nary a creak.

■ **The Point**. When the British Colonial Office in London laid out the plan for the town of Beaufort in 1711, it chose the highest point of land on Port Royal Island facing due south overlooking the water, today known as the residential area of Bay Street. To the east was a low mosquito-infested place, separated from the original town by a small, muddy creek. Over the years, townspeople connected this point of low land to the town by filling in the creek with dirt (no longer allowed by the environmental laws, but a favorite activity in the good old days). Venturesome settlers built small country houses there, and when some of them became filthy rich growing cotton in the mid-1800s, they built large mansions there. Today, this area is called the Point. And the point for some people is to live on the Point.

Ladies and gentlemen in antebellum Beaufort boarded carriages from these steps in front of B.B. Sams' walled mansion on the Point.

■ **Yankees**. The first of about 30,000 of this demonstrative race from up North, dressed in blue uniforms, staged a seaborne invasion here on November 7, 1861, and stayed throughout the Civil War. They and their descendants have been here ever since. They had the cleverness to tax all of the absent Rebels out of their land, thereby assuring that Yankees would forever own a good bit of this heaven called Beaufort. More and more of them keep coming here too, and some of them still like to raise taxes. Yankees seem to like this place. Beaufortonians of the Southern variety have, for the most part, decided they like Yankees too.

Joint Resolution of Congress

A resolution tendering the thanks of Congress to Captain Samuel F. Du Pont and officers, petty officers, seamen, and marines under his command for the victory at Port Royal:

That the thanks of Congress be, and they are hereby, tendered to Captain Samuel F. Du Pont, and through him to the officers, petty officers, seamen, and marines attached to the squadron under his command, for the decisive and splendid victory achieved at Port Royal on the seventh day of November last.

Approved, Washington, D.C., February 22, 1862

George Trask

Arcaded basements, raised entirely above ground level, are a feature of antebellum houses in the Beaufort style.

Beaufort's History

BEAUFORT HAS BEEN A DESTINATION since pre-historic times when nomadic aboriginal tribes first discovered how pleasant it was to spend winters on the islands here. These American Indians left permanent evidence of their settlements in the form of shell rings, dating from the second millennium B.C. The Indian Hill site on St. Helena Island and the Little Barnwell Island site on the Whale Branch River are important archeological finds that historians believe were religious temples. Many of the local roads originated as Indian trails including Beaufort's main thoroughfare, U.S. Highway 21, leading from Garden's Corner to Fripp Island. Old-timers can still remember the part of it running from the ferry at Whale Branch to town as "the old shell road," surfaced with hard-packed oyster shells from the ancient Indian shell mounds.

One of the great joys of childhood in Beaufort has been collecting Indian artifacts. Plowed fields often revealed flint arrowheads, pottery, and pipe stems. Oyster shells packed along a creek bank were a sure sign that, hundreds of years ago, Indians feasted there. The Beaufort Museum now holds many of these ancient relics. Indian mounds also provided the raw material for tabby houses here, the most enduring of the old building materials.

Early Explorers

Beaufort and the surrounding coastal areas to the south including St. Augustine, Florida, about 150 miles away, were among the first to be explored by Europeans and settled in the New World. The Spanish, the French, the English, and the Scots were all interested in the area because of rich soil, abundant natural resources, and proximity to the West Indies, which provided a viable trade route to Europe. These various European explorations affected the culture of the Beaufort area in every facet of life: in names, in architecture, in speech, in agriculture, and in trade of goods from all over the world.

In the second landing of Europeans on the North American continent, the Spanish explored the Beaufort area under the leadership of Pedro de Salazar in 1514. In 1521 a Spanish fleet sailed into Port Royal Sound, surveyed the area, and named it Punta de Santa Elena, which has since been anglicized to St. Helena. This name is now borne by St. Helena Island, St. Helena Sound, St. Helena's Parish, and St. Helena's Church, all in Beaufort county.

The Spanish fleet returned to Florida without establishing a settlement here. Then in 1562, Jean Ribaut, a French Huguenot, established a small settlement called Charlesfort almost within eyesight of what is now downtown Beaufort, the first

---

Whitsontide, Sunday, May 17, 1562

Being of the opynion that there was no fayrer or fytter place for the purpose then porte Royall, when we had sounded the entrey and the channell, (thanked be God) we entred salfely therin with our shippes agenst the opynyon of many, fynding the same one of the greatest and fayrest havens of the worlde.... In this porte are many armes of the sea depe and lardg, and here and there of all sides many rivers of a meane biggnes, where withowt danger all the shippes in the worlde myght be harbored.

—Jean Ribaut, *The Whole & True Discoverye of Terra Florida*, ©1927 Florida State Historical Society

Protestant settlement in North America. It was Ribaut who gave the name Port Royal to this area.

Disease, lack of supplies, and the threat of attack by both Indians and Spaniards soon led the French colonists to abandon the settlement and its fortification. They sailed back across the Atlantic Ocean on a terrible journey that included casting lots to survive. Two years later the Spanish returned and established a settlement at Santa Elena. But Indian uprisings and French and English threats forced them to withdraw after 21 years.

Without a significant Spanish presence here, England laid claim to the area in 1629. But it was not until 1670 that the English sent an expedition to Carolina. Under the leadership of William Sayle, this expedition came to Port Royal but did not settle here for fear of harassment by pirates and Spanish rovers based in nearby Florida. The English instead continued north and founded Charles Town (Charleston), the first English settlement in South Carolina.

Fifteen years later, in 1685, a small band of Scottish Covenanters found Port Royal a more inviting area and established Stuart Town here. This colony was located just about a mile and a half from what is now downtown Beaufort, due south down the river. In 1686 the Spanish attacked and destroyed this Scottish settlement in retaliation for arming and inciting the Yemassee Indians against them.

Permanent Settlement

The area finally became permanently settled when the English crown decided to erect a seaport town here, named after the Duke of Beaufort. Beaufort was chartered in 1711, which makes it the second oldest town in South Carolina and among the earliest towns along the Eastern Seaboard. The British colonial office laid out the town with a grid pattern of streets that remains the same today with Bay Street paralleling the waterfront and side streets leading to the water.

With the chartering of Beaufort, the Anglican Church established St. Helena's Parish in 1712. In 1715 the nearby Yemassee Indians almost annihilated the settlers in the Yemassee War. Corruption in commerce between the settlers and the Indians increased tensions and led to this bloody massacre, with the only surviving colonists narrowly escaping by boat to Charleston. St. Helena's church building still stands today in a full town block, though only part of it is the original structure built in 1724 after the threat of the Indians subsided.

Principal industries in Beaufort during colonial days were indigo and rice. Indigo was valued for its use as a dye for textiles, a burgeoning industry in Europe. The darker the blue in the indigo dye, the greater its value. The Stuart family trans-

Beaufort, July 22, 1724

To the Lord Bishop of London:

We, Your Lordships most dutifull and affectionate people of said parish, beg leave to represent to Your Lordship that we have been an erected parish for above ten years, but through the misfortune of an Indian warr have been without the blessing of having either church or minister. Now it has pleased God to restore us to the blessing of peace, by the bounty of the General Assembly and subscriptions of His Excellency and several other persons have a handsome brick church, a building which will be finisht in three months. Our humble petition to Your Lordship is that Your Lordship would be pleased to send us a sober and learned person to be our minister.

—Church Wardens of St. Helena Parish

formed Cane, Cat, and Gibbes Islands into the most profitable indigo plantations in South Carolina on the eve of the Revolution. John Evans made Orange Grove plantation into the largest indigo plantation on St. Helena Island.

Rice was also profitably farmed in this mild, humid climate in the upper reaches of the tidal areas. The Bull, Barnwell, and Fuller families held large tracts of low-lying wetlands in the Sheldon area. You can still see evidence of massive dikes there, built to regulate the flow of fresh water into the rice fields.

Vast supplies of cypress, live oak, and long-leaf yellow pine proliferated in the area, enabling shipbuilding to become a principal industry here before the American Revolution. Between 1764 and 1774, nearly a dozen operators built about 30 ships ranging in size up to 260 tons for the trans-Atlantic and West Indian trade. They bore romantic names reminiscent of the Lowcountry and of faraway places: *Rose Island, Pallas, Countess of Dumfries, Ashley-Cooper,* and *Live-Oak.*

Trade brought prosperity. Well-heeled merchants, businessmen, and plantation owners settled in Beaufort and built handsome town mansions, such as William Elliott (1103 Bay Street) and John Barnwell (Barnwell Castle, destroyed by fire). Some Beaufort leaders had political aspirations. Thomas Heyward, whose plantation was located near Beaufort, was a leading South Carolina patriot and one of the signers of the *Declaration of Independence.*

Many of the socially prominent families remained loyal to the king. Beaufort became known as a haven of political conservatism, a tendency that doomed the society and wealth of these landowners in a later war. During the Revolution the area was occupied by British troops, a precursor of the Federal occupation during the Civil War. British soldiers from the Revolutionary War were buried in St. Helena's graveyard. The dead of the later war, mostly Union soldiers, occupy an entire National Cemetery here.

Toasts to American Independence

Beaufort, S.C., July 6, 1819

The following toasts were drank on the 5th inst. at the celebration of the anniversary of American Independence by a number of citizens of Beaufort:

1. The Fourth of July—The Day that Liberty consecrates to herself; let tyrants tremble at the thought.

2. Independence—Our sacred heritage, 'twas achieved by the blood of our fathers; by our own will it be defended.

3. The memory of Washington—The records of departed worth furnish not his parallel, and time as it increases the number of contrasts adds lustre to his character.

4. The Constitution of the United States—Embodying the accumulated wisdom of ages, may it become the political creed of every American.

5. The Federal Union—May it receive daily strength by an increasing unanimity of sentiment and feeling.

—*Carolina Gazette* of Charleston, S.C.

Beaufortonians celebrated the Federal union in the early decades of the 19th century. Later, they changed their minds.

Antebellum Days

After the American Revolution, Beaufort's economy became renowned for its long-staple Sea Island cotton, considered the finest cotton in the world. Scientific planters such as the Elliotts and the Barnwells saved the seed from the best cotton plants each year, building up the stock of the superior strain of fiber. Eli Whitney's 1793 invention of the cotton gin on a nearby plantation on the Savannah River helped increase Sea Island cotton production to millions of pounds a year. Money begot larger houses, constructed along the high bluff on Bay Street by Edward Barnwell (1405 Bay Street), John Joyner Smith (400 Wilmington Street), Thomas and Elizabeth Fuller (1211 Bay Street), Robert Means (1207 Bay Street), John Cuthbert (1203 Bay Street), and John Mark Verdier (801 Bay Street).

During the early years of the American republic politicians connected with Beaufort strode the national and the international scenes. Pierce Butler, who held large landholdings here, became the first U.S. senator from South Carolina under the new Federal Constitution. Henry William DeSaussure, a friend of George Washington, became the first director of the United States Mint. Revolutionary War General Charles Cotesworth Pinckney, owner of a large plantation near Hilton Head, became President Washington's minister to France in 1796 and was the Federalist candidate for President in 1804 and 1808.

In 1795 the town's leading citizens founded Beaufort College, one of the first civic educational institutions in the South. In 1807 they incorporated the Beaufort Library Society, which amassed one of the finest book collections in the South until its destruction in the cauldron of the Civil War. Milton Maxcy, a New Englander, founded a private primary school here to give a basic formal education to the sons of the plantation owners, in anticipation that they would go to college up East or in England. Continental visitors to America included Beaufort on their tours, arriving by ship on coastal voyages from Boston, New York, and Philadelphia. William Elliott III, William J. Grayson, and Richard Fuller wrote books and poetry that gained national attention.

The cotton planters in the Sea Islands experienced tremendous wealth in these decades leading up to the Civil War. Construction of a summer mansion on the Point became a mark of distinction for Lewis Reeve Sams (601 Bay Street), Dr. Joseph Johnson ("The Castle"), Edward Means (604 Pinckney Street), Paul Hamilton ("The Oaks"), Berners Barnwell Sams (201 Laurens Street), Edgar Fripp ("Tidalholm"), and other Lowcountry cotton tycoons.

Grand parties and gatherings were an expression of these prosperous times, and homes were built then for entertaining as much as for living. So popular was the town as a watering place for the rich that Beaufort became known as the "Newport of the South" among wealthy plantation owners who shuttled between the real Newport in Rhode Island and its counterpart here in Beaufort, South Carolina. Sons of the wealthy went to Harvard, Yale, and Edinburgh for their education; daughters went to Newport for their sweethearts and husbands. Beaufort was the epitome of the high society of the Old South, and its downfall was, indeed, the true story of *Gone With the Wind*.

Civil War

Because of Beaufort's insularity and its dependence on a plantation economy, it was home to a number of South Carolina's most vociferous states' rights firebrands. Beaufortonian Robert Barnwell Rhett was especially vocal in advocating secession from the Union. He drafted the first Ordinance of Secession here in 1860 in what is now known as Secession House (1113 Craven Street). Secession from the Union proved disastrous to South Carolina and the entire South. In an exquisite irony, it was most disastrous to the cotton planters of Beaufort.

The war began in April 1861 with the Rebels shelling Fort Sumter in Charleston harbor. To wage war against the South, the Union needed a secure port, bivouac area, and coaling station on the South Atlantic coast. Because of its central location on the coast, its deep-water anchorages, and its isolation from the mainland, Port Royal was the chosen target.

Flag-Officer Samuel F. Du Pont led the South Atlantic Blockading Squadron's invasion fleet from his frigate *Wabash*. Seventeen steam-powered frigates and gunboats sailed from

Beaufort, S.C., Oct 16th, 1862.

The 'city' of Beaufort, as it was called by its former inhabitants, must have been a very beautiful place previous to its occupancy by our Soldiers. It is finely located on the Beaufort river—which forms a graceful curve somewhat crescent shaped, very inviting to the eye as we approach the place.... Previous to the landing of our troops there were well kept yards and beautiful gardens, full of rare flowers—Mansions furnished with almost princely magnificense—whole libraries full of costly books—indeed, this little place contained everything which art could furnish and wealth procure.

—Esther Hill Hawk's diary, *A Woman Doctor's Civil War*, Gerald Schwartz, editor, © 1984 University of South Carolina

A native of New Hampshire, Dr. Esther Hawks (1833-1906) wrote a compassionate diary of her Civil War experiences in Beaufort.

Frank Leslie's Illustrated Newspaper, Nov. 23, 1861

Beaufort area, November 7, 1861, showing Federal ships massed for invasion of the Sea Islands, bringing 30,000 Union troops.

Hampton Roads, Virginia, on October 29, 1861, bound for Port Royal. A convoy of 33 U.S. Army transport ships followed, under the command of U.S. Brigadier-General Thomas W. Sherman (*not* the General William Tecumseh Sherman of later Union fame). The transports carried 12,000 U.S. army soldiers, the first of a force of 30,000 troops that landed on Beaufort's shores. An additional 25 coaling vessels accompanied the fleet. In all, it was the largest U.S. naval landing until the Normandy invasion of 1944.

The cataclysm for the Southern planters on the Sea Islands, remembered by their former slaves as the "Day of the Big Gun Shoot," began at 9:26 a.m. on a calm and crystal-clear autumn morning, November 7, 1861. Coming six months after Fort Sumter's fall, this was one of the first great Union military operations of the Civil War. The naval force hurled itself into Port Royal Sound, cannons blazing against the sand-fortified embankments of the poorly-constructed Confederate defenses at Fort Walker (Hilton Head Island) and Fort Beauregard (Bay Point). The motley force of defending Confederates gave up after a four-hour fight. Total Union casualties were eight men killed and 23 wounded. The Confederates lost 11 men killed and 48 wounded. In one relatively bloodless day the Union forces occupied the Sea Islands.

The town of Beaufort escaped damage due to the propitious Union outcome. Warned by Southern spies in New York and Washington who telegraphed the Federal invasion plan, every white person here, except one drunkard, fled. Most never returned after the war, four long years later. Beaufort immediately became as thoroughly Union territory as the deepest reaches of Boston, New York, and Philadelphia. Suddenly, Beaufort was a Northern place.

With no time to prepare against the invasion, the fleeing white Southerners took only necessities and left their homes almost entirely intact. They also left behind 10,000 slaves on their

Sea Island plantations and at their mansions in town. Union troops rescued the homes from rampant plundering by the abandoned slaves. On the mainland at Coosawhatchie, a small detachment of Confederate soldiers helped the fleeing whites to evacuate the area. The Rebel commander there was a little-known Virginian who was later to gain great fame: General Robert E. Lee.

Beaufort became a hospital zone and a Union army regional headquarters throughout the war. Injured Union soldiers were brought here from battlegrounds throughout the South because Beaufort was safe territory and easily accessible by sea. St. Helena's Episcopal Church and The Baptist Church of Beaufort both served as hospitals. Tombstones were used as operating tables.

Frank Leslie's Illustrated Newspaper, Jan. 11, 1862

Thousands of proud Yankees paraded down Bay Street in late 1861 after invading Beaufort and running the Rebels off the Sea Islands.

In an effort reminiscent of the French Revolution, the Federal occupiers changed the names of the streets in town to letters and numbers. Bay Street, for example, became A Street. The inevitable Thermidorian reaction after the war restored the historical street names.

Many of the houses in the downtown historic district were seized as hospitals or as officers' quarters. General Isaac Ingalls Stevens, who led the invasion troops down Bay Street in a grand parade on December 5, 1861, set up his quarters in the John Joyner Smith house (400 Wilmington Street). The John Mark Verdier House (801 Bay Street) served as a Union army headquarters building. When the houses were auctioned by the U.S. Federal Direct Tax Commission in 1864, General Rufus Saxton, commander of the Department of the South, purchased for $2,000 the John A. Cuthbert House (1203 Bay Street) as his residence. The Reverend Mansfield French, head

Dear Mother,

This is an odd sort of place. All the original inhabitants are gone—and the houses are occupied by Northerners.

Your loving son,

Robert Gould Shaw
Beaufort, June 6, 1863

—*Blue-Eyed Child of Fortune: the Civil War Letters of Colonel Robert Gould Shaw*, edited by Russell Duncan, ©1992 University of Georgia Press

Colonel Shaw, martyred in nearby battle, commanded the famous Massachusetts 54th Regiment of black soldiers in the Civil War.

of the missionaries sent to help the freed slaves, bought the Fuller mansion (1211 Bay Street) for $1800.

During the war tens of thousands of soldiers from Northern states—Maine, New Hampshire, Vermont, Massachusetts, Rhode Island, Connecticut, New York, New Jersey, Pennsylvania, West Virginia, Ohio, Indiana, Illinois, Michigan, Wisconsin, Minnesota, Iowa—were transported here by ship for encampment and final training before moving out to battle. The first black regiments, including the famous Massachusetts 54th commanded by Colonel Robert Gould Shaw, called Beaufort home during the war. The National Cemetery on Boundary Street, established during the wartime occupation, is filled with battlefield dead from the Union states. In a small corner of the cemetery lie the remains of 200 Confederate soldiers.

Frank Leslie's Illustrated Newspaper, Jan. 24, 1863

The color-sergeant of the 1st Regiment S.C. Volunteers addressed the crowd at Beaufort on Emancipation Day, January 1, 1863.

The first great experiments in freedom for the black people began here in early 1862 when Northern missionaries arrived to care for and to teach the abandoned slaves, pointing the way to the Emancipation Proclamation and the 14th Amendment to the Constitution. On January 1, 1863, the Emancipation Proclamation was read to the freedmen in a joyous celebration on the Sea Islands, the only area to which the proclamation initially applied.

Following emancipation the U.S. Government imposed a Federal real estate tax on the land and homes here. The Southern owners being absent and unable to pay the tax, the Federal

---

St. Helena Island, Thursday, New Year's Day, 1863 [Emancipation Day]

The most glorious day this nation has yet seen, *I* think .... We stopped at Beaufort, then proceeded to Camp Saxton, the camp of the 1st Regiment South Carolina Volunteers.... I cannot give a regular chronicle of the day. It is impossible. I was in such a state of excitement. It all seemed, and seems still, like a brilliant dream.... I thought I had never seen a sight so beautiful. There were the black soldiers, in their blue coats and scarlett pants, the officers of this and other regiments in their handsome uniforms, and crowds of lookers-on, men, women and children, grouped in various attitudes, under the trees. The faces all wore a happy, eager, expectant look.

—*The Journal of Charlotte L. Forten, edited by Ray Allen Billington, © 1953 The Dryden Press, Inc.*

Charlotte Forten (1838-1914) was a well-educated black Philadelphian who worked as a missionary among the freedmen on St. Helena Island.

government confiscated the land. The homes in town were auctioned to the occupying Union soldiers and civilians, and many of the plantations were cut into 40-acre tracts and sold for nominal sums to the newly freed slaves. In this way, at a price of $2.00 per acre, freedmen were able to buy 40 acres and a mule. As a result, black residents became self-sufficient landowning small farmers here, not tenant farmers.

Quakers from Philadelphia established Penn Normal School, named in honor of William Penn, as a trade school for the freedmen on St. Helena Island, teaching them how to work as independent farmers on the land they had acquired. The campus of the first school for black people, now called Penn Center, is still in existence today on St. Helena Island and is

St. Helenaville, Thursday, November 17, 1864

The weather is exquisite, [Penn] school flourishing, household matters comfortable, living good, and all things smooth at present.... We have a very large school and a charming time in it. Just think, you poor, freezing, wind-pierced mortals! *We* have summer weather. The fields are gay with white, purple, and yellow flowers, and with the red leaves of sumach and other shrubs. Our woods are always green, and just now the gum trees make them beautiful with red. *You* can't see a leaf! Chill November! I pity you.

—*Letters and Diary of Laura M. Towne, written from the Sea Islands of South Carolina, 1862-1884,* edited by Rupert Sargent Holland, 1912

Laura Towne (1825-1901) and her friend Ellen Murray devoted their lives to Penn School and the people of St. Helena Island.

open to the public. Black land ownership and racial toleration
became a hallmark of this area, presaging the modern-day celebration here of the Gullah culture.

General William Tecumseh Sherman, generally regarded as
the scourge of the South, smiled broadly on Beaufort. Rather
than engaging in his usual incendiary habits, he merely took a
boat ride over from Savannah after his march through Georgia
to visit his Union army friends headquartered here. Before em-
barking on his ruinous campaign through rebellious South
Carolina in early 1865, General Sherman spent the night at his
friend General Rufus Saxton's house on Bay Street.

Agriculture and Military Economy

During the decades following the Civil War, the black pop-
ulation of the Sea Islands outnumbered the whites seven to
one. Robert Smalls, a Beaufortonian who had been a slave and
then a Civil War hero to the Union, became one of the first
black U.S. Congressmen and served a long and prominent political career after the war. He first made a name for himself in
1862 by stealing a Confederate gunboat from Charleston harbor and sailing it to safe Union territory in his home town of
Beaufort. The main highway leading into town from the direction of Savannah and a large public high school are named after
him. A statue on Craven Street next to Tabernacle Baptist
Church commemorates his many accomplishments.

The Civil War military occupation of the Beaufort area
proved disastrous to cotton cultivation here. Not understanding the necessity for the hand selection of the superior seeds at
the end of each season for the next year's planting, the Union
occupiers sent all of the 1862 harvest to New York for ginning,
losing instantly the superior strain of cotton seed. And what the
Yankees didn't destroy, the boll weevil in later years did destroy. Thus ended Sea Island cotton.

Discovery in the 1870s of phosphate deposits here created excitement that mining of this raw material might prove the salvation of the local economy. A railroad spur was built from Yemassee on the mainland to the southern tip of Port Royal Island, the genesis of the small town of Port Royal at the end of the spur. But the phosphate was soon depleted, and larger deposits were found in Florida.

One of the most memorable and tragic events of the century occurred in 1893, when a fearsome hurricane, perhaps the strongest storm in recorded history here, struck without warning. More than 2,000 people drowned when the storm pushed a tidal wave over low-lying areas. Clara Barton, Joel Chandler Harris, and a host of other notables arrived to provide disaster relief and to announce the tragedy to the world.

With the establishment of a U.S. Naval Station on Parris Island in 1891, Beaufort began to experience the role the modern military would play in its economy. In World War I the installation became a U.S. Marine training facility, now the Marine Corps Recruit Depot Parris Island. In 1942 a U.S. Naval Air Station was established on farmland at Grays Hill that became the Marine Corps Air Station Beaufort. These bases, together with the U.S. Naval Hospital Beaufort, have pumped hundreds of millions of dollars into the local economy. In addition to 15,000 active-duty military personnel and their families currently stationed here, thousands of retired military people have chosen Beaufort as home.

Beginning in the early 20th century, truck farming became a major part of the economy, supplanting the failed cotton. Large farms on Port Royal Island, St. Helena Island, Cane Island, Cat Island, and Distant Island produced as many as 35 different varieties of fresh vegetables in three seasons annually, summer being the only time when the weather was too hot for growing vegetables commercially. Thousands of inhabitants on the islands held employment during the Great Depression when the agricultural economies in other areas had been decimated. Names still prominent in the community—among them Trask, Sanders, McLeod, Bellamy, John Gray—attest to the enduring influence of the agricultural families. Truck farming has continued, especially tomatoes on large tracts of land on St. Helena Island, but not nearly to the extent of prior decades.

Commercial fishing, shrimping, and oystering also became an important part of Beaufort's economy in the first half of the 20th century. Though the seafood industry is clearly on the wane here, you may still see commercial shrimp boats moored at the Gay family dock along the creek as you drive from St. Helena to Hunting Island. And a few Gullah oystermen still ply the creeks to load their flat-bottom boats with mounds of fresh oysters.

George Trask

Proud Beaufort farmers stand in 1955 in a field of iceberg lettuce on Cat Island, ready for harvesting and shipment to New York City.

Tourism and Retirement

In spite of the disaster of the Civil War, the town never lost its charm as a social watering spot. General Rufus Saxton's military headquarters (1015 Bay Street) was converted into the Sea Island Hotel and was operated by the family of Maude Odell, a famous Broadway actress. The Thomas Fuller House (1211 Bay Street) was renamed "Tabby Manse" by the Onthank family, its post-Civil-War owners from Boston, and operated as a wintertime retreat for wealthy Northerners. Tidalholm on the Point became a similar retreat.

Perhaps the most famous watering spot was at the corner of Bay and New Streets, the now-demolished Gold Eagle Tavern, an internationally-known place to eat and sleep during the first

Gold Eagle Tavern in its heyday as a mecca for sophisticated Northerners wintering on the Bay in Beaufort.

half of the 20th century. It was named after the first gold dollars, called gold eagles, issued by the United States Mint during the presidency of George Washington. The director of the mint had been a Beaufortonian and friend of Washington named Henry William DeSaussure.

In recent decades retirement communities and tourism have replaced the traditional ways to make a living from Beaufort's proximity to the sea. Hilton Head Island in the southern part of Beaufort county, until 1955 an isolated backwater without a bridge to the mainland, led the way with Charles Fraser's development of Sea Pines Plantation. A bridge to Fripp Island soon followed, with its development also as an oceanfront community. Since the 1960s thousands of newcomers have taken up residence in planned communities on Lady's, Fripp, Cat, Brays, Callawassie, and Spring Islands, as well as in the Hilton Head and Bluffton areas.

Almost all of the newcomers arrive without understanding of the rich history and traditions of the area but they soon recognize, in common with the long-time residents, its uniqueness. A defining moment occurred in 1970 when BASF, a German chemical manufacturer, sought to build a petroleum-cracking plant in the county. The hue and cry from outraged Lowcountry residents forced the company to abandon its plans. This event set the course of Beaufort county as perhaps the only east-coast county without a significant industrial plant.

Today the Beaufort area is changing as more and more people discover its charms. Rural land is being converted into residential communities and shopping centers. Tranquillity is being replaced by traffic. As the economy continues to change, Beaufortonians, both old-timers and newcomers, seek vigilantly to maintain the natural environment and the small-town ambiance that make Beaufort a special place so that Beaufort will not become just another place.

George Trask

Swings frame the view of boats moored at the city marina, which is adjacent to the downtown waterfront park.

A Tour of Beaufort's Historic District

BEAUFORT IS A TOWN ON AN ISLAND, and the town is defined by its proximity to the sea. The downtown historic district encompasses the boundaries of the old town, focused on the waterfront facing due south. Some of the houses date back to the early 1700s, the time when the town was chartered by the British crown. Almost all of them have outstanding features.

Ample parking for your car is available downtown. The best way to see old Beaufort is by strolling. The historic district is relatively small, easily traversed on foot. If you would like a personally guided walking tour, check at the Greater Beaufort Chamber of Commerce Visitors' Center, corner of Carteret and Boundary Streets. Or you may wish to see the old parts of town on a bicycle, available for rent at Best Western Sea Island Inn, 1015 Bay Street. A particularly fun way is a horse-drawn carriage tour with its leisurely pace and knowledgeable guide. There are several carriage outfits, which also conduct guided tours in minibuses.

Be sure to take enough time to savor the ambiance of the downtown historic district. Stroll or ride in front of the grand houses on Bay Street facing due south on the high bluff; explore the Point to the east with its narrow side streets running to the water. In between is the downtown shopping district with lots of specialty shops, restaurants, the waterfront park, and the downtown marina.

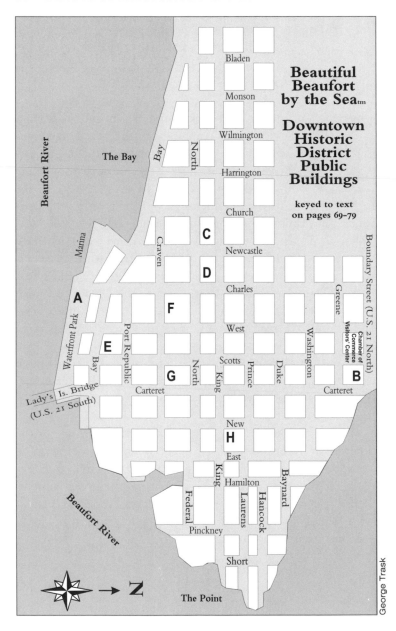

Public Buildings

■ **A. Waterfront Park and Downtown Marina**. The city's waterfront park with handsome trees and a panoramic view looking south over the Bay was designed by renowned landscape architect Robert Marvin, who practices his craft in his nearby hometown of Walterboro, South Carolina. The park has picnic areas, a seasonal farmer's market on Saturdays, and a covered pavilion that features concerts, art shows, and local events throughout the year. A large playground for children and swings on the waterfront for their parents take in the view as well. Not to be missed. Enter the park from various locations along Bay Street or at the foot of the Lady's Island Bridge. The porches of a number of the restaurants on Bay Street face the park, a most pleasant place to dine or to sip an afternoon refreshment.

At the west end of the park is the downtown marina, a city-owned facility leased to a local private operator. The marina provides berths for watercraft plying the Intracoastal Waterway, which range in size from outboard motorboats to grand sailing and motor yachts.

■ **B. Greater Beaufort Chamber of Commerce Visitors' Center, 1106 Carteret Street.** Formerly located at the western end of the waterfront park near the downtown marina, the Visitors' Center has recently moved to a new location at the corner of Carteret and Boundary Streets, more spacious but less convenient to downtown. This is the place for visitors and residents to begin their visit to the Beaufort area. Tour maps, tour books, information about community events, promotions of local businesses, friendly and knowledgeable staff, and tickets for carriage and boat tours are just a few of the benefits of a visit here. Open daily and Sundays.

George Trask

■ **C. St. Helena's Episcopal Church, 507 Newcastle Street,** parish established 1712, bounded by North, Church, King and Newcastle Streets. Seat of one of the earliest Anglican parishes established in North America, this church is steeped in history. Only a small portion of the building itself is original (1724) because it was expanded over the years to meet the needs of the growing congregation. The structure you see today, which is on the verge of a major renovation, was essentially complete no later than the mid-1800s. The steeple appears to be as old as the building; it is a 20th-century addition.

During the Civil War, Union army surgeons removed the pews to convert the sanctuary into a Union hospital. Amputations were performed on the gravestones. The altar was replaced by an ornate wooden altar carved by sailors on the *U.S.S. New Hampshire*, a Federal warship stationed here during Reconstruction. The Taylor and Booty organ, considered to be one of the finest Dutch-style organs in America, was added to the balcony in the early 1980s. It is admired far and wide for its performances of Bach and other classical organ composers.

The churchyard is the burial place of many of Beaufort's prominent early citizens, including "Tuscarora Jack" Barnwell, the famous Indian fighter and forebear of most of Beaufort's antebellum inhabitants. One ancient grave, in the shape of a small brick building, contains the remains of a man who was buried with a candle, a pick, a shovel, and a meal, in hopes that he might not be dead but might dig himself out after a good night's rest and breakfast. Another grave holds the remains of two British soldiers killed here during the American Revolution, and yet another the remains of Mason Locke Weems, the itinerant cleric and amateur historian who in 1806 invented the story of George Washington chopping down the cherry tree. A short history of the church with anecdotes about the graveyard can be purchased from the parish office on Newcastle Street.

George Trask

■ **D. The Baptist Church of Beaufort, 600 Charles Street.** This stately Greek Revival structure was constructed in 1844 under the ministry of the great Dr. Richard Fuller. A Beaufort native educated at Harvard, Fuller renounced his law practice in 1831 to become the Baptist minister to 3,500 slaves in a congregation of less than 200 whites. He helped found the Southern Baptist Convention, wrote a number of well-known religious tracts, and gained national prominence. In 1846 he anticipated the coming of the Civil War and removed himself to Baltimore, Maryland, where he built three additional churches and baptized Annie Armstrong, the patron saint of Baptist philanthropy. When the Civil War came, he served as an intermediary between President Lincoln and the Southern leadership. Today, 125 years after his death, he is still revered by the people of Beaufort and of Baltimore.

Inside and outside, the structure closely resembles First Baptist Church in Charleston, designed in 1822 by Robert Mills, a South Carolinian who was America's first trained architect and the designer of the Washington Monument. During the Civil War pews were removed and scattered so that the church could serve as a hospital. Providentially, the pews were recovered and restored, as was the communion table. In 1959, Hurricane Gracie blew the roof off. Again, providence intervened and the ornamental plaster ceiling was saved. A recent major renovation has extended the choir and installed an impressive pipe organ.

The steeple, erected in 1961, is the highest point above ground level in downtown Beaufort. It can be seen from miles away on the waterfront approaches to town. The graveyard surrounding the structure contains numerous stately trees and has served as a final resting place for more than 150 years. The church is open to the public for viewing as well as worship. Friendly, knowledgeable docents are available to give you a tour and tell you about its history.

George Trask

■ **E. John Mark Verdier House, 801 Bay Street.** A meticulously restored house museum owned and operated by Historic Beaufort Foundation, this structure is open to the public for scheduled tours lasting about 45 minutes. It also contains a gift shop with cards, books, and gifts from Beaufort. Tour brochures and schedules are also available at the Greater Beaufort Chamber of Commerce Visitors' Center.

Built about 1790 by Beaufort's merchant prince, John Mark Verdier, soon after the end of the Revolutionary War, the Verdier house displays antiques from the Federal period, some of which belonged to Verdier himself. The Marquis de Lafayette, the beloved Frenchman who fought with General George Washington during the American Revolution, spoke from the front steps here on his famous visit to America in 1825. Ever since then, this house has also been called the Lafayette house.

The house served as a Union army headquarters building during the Civil War. Afterwards it became a commercial structure, used over the years for such colorful and varied activities as a local telephone exchange, a fish market, an ice house, a law office, a restaurant, and a barber shop. In the 1960s, under the leadership of Howard Danner and Riley Gettys, Historic Beaufort Foundation was formed to promote the preservation and restoration of Beaufort's architectural heritage. In 1968 the foundation purchased the Verdier house to serve as its headquarters and as a house museum. After a successful capital campaign the foundation restored the Verdier house, opened it to the public in 1976, and set the citizens of Beaufort on a course of formal appreciation for the outstanding collection of 18th- and 19th-century houses here.

George Trask

■ **F. Tabernacle Baptist Church, 907 Craven Street.** Before the Civil War, white and black Baptists worshipped under the umbrella of The Baptist Church of Beaufort, located a block away on Charles Street. The congregation of that church, led by Dr. Richard Fuller, included 3,500 black slaves in addition to the 200 white members. In the 1840s, these Baptists built "The Tabernacle" on Craven Street as a lecture room and meeting house. The Civil War split the congregation into separate organizations, which have continued to the present day. In 1863 the Reverend Solomon Peck of Boston led 500 black members out of the church on Charles Street. At the end of the war they purchased "The Tabernacle" as their own separate church.

In the churchyard is the grave and a monument to the memory of Robert Smalls (1839-1915), the ex-slave from Beaufort who captured at Charleston the Confederate gunboat *Planter* in January 1862 and delivered it to the occupying Union forces here. A loyal Republican, during and after Reconstruction Smalls served as the most outstanding black politician in South Carolina. In 1869 he became a representative of the Beaufort district in the state legislature. In 1870 he rose to become a state senator. In 1871 the governor appointed him a brigadier general in command of a brigade of the South Carolina national guard. In 1875 he entered the U.S. Congress, representing the fifth district of South Carolina until defeated by William Elliott in a contested election in 1886. For the next 20 years he served as the U.S. port collector at Beaufort.

During the Civil War auction of Beaufort properties, Smalls purchased the home of his ex-slavemaster, Henry McKee. When McKee's widow became destitute and ill after the war, Smalls took her into his house (her former home) and cared for her. When his fellow Republican politicians in Beaufort became corrupt, Smalls opposed them.

■ **G. The Arsenal and the Beaufort Museum, 713 Craven Street.** When Beaufort was founded in 1711, the British colonial office laid out the town square at the nearby intersection of Craven and Carteret Streets. This site became the colonial courthouse. At the beginning of the American Revolution in 1775, the patriots organized the Beaufort Volunteer Artillery here, the fifth military unit established in what became the United States of America. In 1795, after the courthouse was removed, the Artillery built this castellated military structure as its headquarters, later distinguishing itself on the side of the Confederacy in the Civil War. The structure now houses the Beaufort Museum. The exterior sports a yellow lime wash, a historical reference to its antebellum hue, intended to bring lightness and cheer to this part of Craven Street.

George Trask

■ **H. First African Baptist Church, 601 New Street.** The First African Baptist Church, constructed in 1865 just as the Civil War ended, stands on the Point as a symbol of the continuing faith of black Baptists. In addition to weekly worship services, this coastal vernacular structure is the scene of musical events such as performances by the Hallelujah Singers, a popular local Gullah group that sings spirituals. Paul Robeson, the celebrated black bass-baritone singer and political activist, performed a concert here in the 1930s.

George Trask

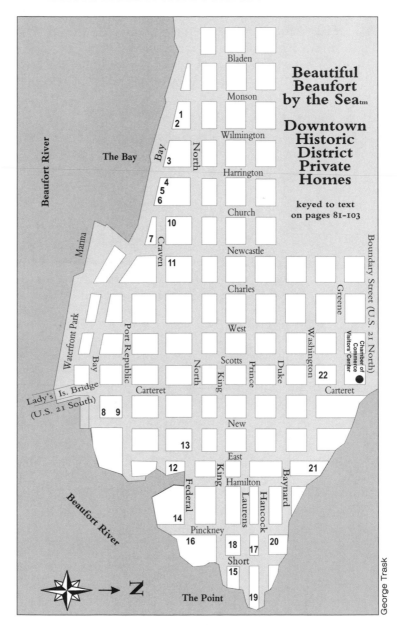

Beautiful Beaufort by the Seatm

Downtown Historic District Private Homes

keyed to text on pages 81-103

Private Homes

The oldest neighborhoods in Beaufort, on the Bay and on the Point, compose a collection of some the most outstanding early residences in America. All of the old houses face south in order to catch the cooling sea breezes in summer and the warming southern sun in winter. The relationship of the houses to street or water does not determine the front; the front always faces south. Almost all of the houses are built on a raised basement. Many have rear wings projecting in a T pattern to allow back rooms a breeze and a view of the water. These features, together with expansive porches across the fronts and in some cases wrapping around the sides, have come together in a most pleasant way to be known as the "Beaufort style."

In spite of the relatively large number of antebellum mansions in the historic district, only about a dozen directly face the water. Visitors often inquire about the value of the old homes. Suffice it to say that in recent years some of them have sold for well over a million dollars. The following is a list of some of the more outstanding houses architecturally, all dating before the Civil War and some built more than two centuries ago.

■ **1. Edward Barnwell House, 1785, 1405 Bay Street.** Handsome interior paneling and mantels distinguish the interior of this large frame house overlooking Beaufort Bay. The Barnwell dynasty was founded by "Tuscarora Jack" Barnwell (d. 1724), an Irishman who became famous in colonial America by subduing the Indians along coastal South Carolina and in eastern North Carolina. His descendants, including Edward Barnwell (1757-1808) who built this house, became immensely rich from rice, indigo, and cotton. They populated Beaufort in the decades leading up to the Civil War when everyone was related to the Barnwells.

■ **2. John Joyner Smith House, c. 1811, 400 Wilmington Street.** This house was in the Barnwell family by virtue of the fact that John Joyner Smith (1790-1872) of Savannah married Mary Gibbes Barnwell. He grew cotton at Old Fort plantation, the site of what is now the U.S. Naval Hospital. Massive columns create a broad expanse of porches across the entire front of the house. The ornate front door facing Bay Street, south in the proper "Beaufort style," is false. You enter the house up the marble steps on Wilmington Street. Two drawing rooms span the entire front facing the water. General Isaac Ingalls Stevens (1818-1862), who was graduated first in his class from West Point in 1839 and who commanded the 1861 Federal occupation of Beaufort, resided here during the early months of the occupation. He was transferred to Virginia and death on September 1, 1862, at the bloody battle of Chantilly, immediately after the nearby battle of Bull Run. After General Stevens' departure this house became a Civil War hospital.

U.S. General Isaac Ingalls Stevens (seated) and staff on porch of John Joyner Smith's house, 400 Wilmington Street, 1862.

■ **3. Charles Edward Leverett House, pre-Revolutionary, 1301 Bay Street.** Originally located on a plantation on St. Helena Island, this house was moved by Dr. Charles Edward Leverett (1808-1868) to its location close by the sidewalk along Bay Street by barge around 1850. One can imagine the struggles of horses and men hauling this large frame house up the bluff to settle on its brick piers. Its proximity to the street gives grand views of the water. Dr. Leverett, a native of Boston and a graduate of Trinity College in Connecticut, was the last rector of Old Sheldon Church before the Civil War. White picket fences and white-washed tree trunks lined this area of Bay Street in the 1880s. The Lea family lived here for many decades of the 20th century. The house has recently undergone a careful restoration and is now the proud possession of new owners.

Bay Street about 1883 with the Rev. Charles Edward Leverett's house behind the white picket fence.

■ **4. Thomas Fuller House,** *Tabby Manse*, **c. 1786, 1211 Bay Street.** Beloved architectural gem and prototype of houses in the "Beaufort style," Tabby Manse is ranked by architectural historians along with Thomas Jefferson's Monticello as a perfect expression of American Palladian-style architecture. Its delicate front portico and solid tabby walls, covered in stucco scored to look like blocks of stone, distinguish the exterior. But the true beauty of the house is its interior with wide heart-pine flooring, pine and cypress panelling, Adam-style mantels, and perfectly proportioned rooms.

Built by Thomas Fuller (1760-1830) as a wedding gift for his bride, Elizabeth Middleton (1764-1833), the house reflects the wealth of the Middleton family of Charleston. Her first cousin, Arthur Middleton, signed the *Declaration of Independence* on behalf of South Carolina. Her great-grandfather was "Tuscarora

Thomas Fuller house, *Tabby Manse*
c. 1786, 1211 Bay Street

The summer residence of the Fuller family in Beaufort was a fine mansion of tabby (a mixture of shells and small stones) on the south front of the town. The house stands on a commanding bluff, and the river stretches away in front, for miles and miles in an almost unbroken line, towards Port Royal. An enclosure of choice plants, with a grand old sycamore, intervened between the piazza and the front street; while spacious out-buildings, and a garden that yielded delicious oranges, formed the premises in the rear. Such was the home of the happy circle gathered there in the long Southern summer.

— J.H. Cuthbert, *Life of Richard Fuller*, 1879

Jack" Barnwell, founder of the ubiquitous Barnwell dynasty. Thomas and Elizabeth reared their twelve children in this house, two of whom attended Harvard College: Richard Fuller and Dr. Thomas Fuller. Richard particularly distinguished himself as a nationally-renowned Baptist minister.

In 1864 the Reverend Mansfield French (1810-1876), leader of the Northern missionaries who came to educate the newly-freed slaves, purchased the house at the Federal confiscatory auction for $1800. After Mansfield failed in his Reconstruction bid to become a U.S. senator from defeated South Carolina, he departed the state, leaving his son, Winchell (1838-1903), to found Beaufort's first post-Civil-War newspaper here, *The Beaufort Tribune*. In the late 1930s Francis Griswold, wrote *A Sea Island Lady*, a novel in the mold of *Gone With the Wind*, while staying here, describing Tabby Manse as the heart of the house he called "Marshlands." The present occupants are the third family to own Tabby Manse in its entire 200-year history.

5. Robert Means House, c. 1790, 1207 Bay Street. Adam-style panelling and decorative mantels in the two front drawing rooms distinguish the interior of this large, recently-restored waterfront house. It was built by prominent merchant and planter Robert Means (1774-1832), a native of Boston who married Mary Hutson Barnwell. They had twelve children, the eldest of whom died in 1824 during his junior year at Yale. A daughter, Mary, married one of the boys next door at 1211 Bay Street, Henry Middleton Fuller. Robert Means' cotton plantation was located on Parris Island. This house became the home of President Warren Harding's Secretary of the Navy, Edwin Denby, during the 1920s. Denby rebuilt the facade, adding the massive two-story pillars supported on masonry arches. The large lot runs all the way through from Bay to North Street with a rear garden of azaleas and camellias.

George Trask

■ 6. John Alexander Cuthbert House, c. 1810, 1203 Bay Street. The strong classical exterior of this house with its tall central portico blends with numerous Victorian additions on the porches and wings. John Alexander Cuthbert (1790-1817), father of four children, was a Beaufort planter who died at the age of 27 during the great fever epidemic of 1817. Union Army General Rufus Saxton, military governor of the Department of the South, lived here throughout the Civil War, purchasing the house as his own property at the Federal tax auction in 1864. His friend General William Tecumseh Sherman visited Saxton in this house just before Sherman's army departed from Beaufort and Savannah in early 1865 on its infamous march northward through South Carolina. The house has recently become a bed and breakfast inn appropriately named the Cuthbert House.

General W.T. Sherman, nemesis of South Carolina, on his trusty steed at Savannah, December 1864, before visiting friends in Beaufort.

■ **7. William Elliott House,** *The Anchorage,* **pre-Revolutionary, 1103 Bay Street.** The most famous member of the Elliott family, and the man who lived here at the time of the Federal invasion in 1861, was William Elliott III (1788-1863). A Phi Beta Kappa student at Harvard, Elliott became immensely wealthy from 12 cotton plantations. He was a pro-Unionist politician, an internationally-known horticulturist, and an author of national renown. His *Carolina Sports by Land and Water* remains in print today as the most typically American counterpart of Izaac Walton's *The Compleat Angler.* This dignified mansion was massively changed outside and inside by retired U.S. Navy Admiral Beardsley in the early 1900s at a cost of $80,000, equivalent to about $1,500,000 today.

The Anchorage *is one of the antebellum structures in Beaufort individually listed on the National Register of Historic Places.*

■ **8. Lewis Reeve Sams House, 1852, 601 Bay Street.**
Built in the heyday of King Cotton as a summer mansion by
the co-owner (with his brother, B.B. Sams) of Datha Island,
this handsome mid-18th century "Beaufort style" house with
Greek-Revival characteristics features Doric columns on the
lower verandah, Ionic columns above, and handsome marble
steps leading to a wide doorway. So close to the water is the
house that the verandahs feel like the prow of a ship on the high
seas. After the Civil War the sons of Lewis Reeve Sams were
able, unlike most pre-war Beaufort families, to reacquire title
to this house. In 1869 they sold it to George Waterhouse, a
Massachusetts native who became a prosperous and highly respected merchant in post-Civil-War Beaufort. Waterhouse descendants continued to live here until recent decades when the
house became a bed and breakfast inn.

■ **9. Thomas Hepworth House, c. 1717, 214 New Street.**
Second only to Charleston as the most important settlement in
colonial South Carolina, Beaufort was home to many prominent early leaders including the man who built this house,
Thomas Hepworth, chief justice of the colony of South Carolina in the early days of the colony. The oldest remaining house
in Beaufort, it features musket slits in its phosphate-rock foundation to allow the Hepworths to protect themselves from Indians, who were still a real threat when this cottage-style house
was built. The house features dormer windows on both its
north and south elevations, reminiscent of the "House of Seven
Gables" in Salem, Massachusetts. During the Revolutionary
War a British gunboat in Beaufort River fired a cannon that
struck this house, no doubt turning the deceased Chief Justice
Hepworth, a loyal subject of the king, over in his grave. A colorful and outspoken Beaufortonian and his thespian wife,
members of a prolific and energetic local family, recently reno-
vated this house.

■ **10. Milton Maxcy House,** *Secession House,* **c. 1813, 1113 Craven Street.** The Greek revival features of this house exemplify the high quality of the old Beaufort waterfront mansions. Overlooking the Bay across a small park, it features an arcaded basement supporting both Ionic and Corinthian columns, a curved marble entrance staircase, and ornate handwrought ironwork. The interior includes black marble mantels, ornate ceiling plaster, and a mahogany staircase.

The first owner was a native of Massachusetts, Milton Maxcy (1782-1817), who practiced law in Beaufort and founded here a school for boys. His brother, Jonathon Maxcy, served as the second president of Rhode Island College (now Brown University) before becoming the president of South Carolina College in Columbia (now the University of South Carolina). Milton married a local indigo and cotton widow and heiress, Mary Bull. Her father, General Stephen Bull, and her first husband, Nathaniel Barnwell II, were scions of two of Beaufort's wealthiest plantation families.

Much of the classical ornamentation on the house was added by its second owner, Edmund Rhett (1808-1863). A Phi Beta Kappa graduate from Yale College in 1830 who became a state senator, he was a member of the fiery family of Rhetts, wealthy cotton planters and politicians who championed secession of South Carolina from the Union. Edmund's brother, U.S. Congressman Robert Barnwell Rhett, became known as the "father of Secession," and wrote the first draft of South Carolina's Ordinance of Secession from the Union in this house in late 1860. Secession lasted only six months in Beaufort. When the Union soldiers invaded Beaufort in November 1861 they turned the house into a hospital and put the paymaster's office in the basement. Enlisted men standing in line for their pay left graffiti on the basement walls, still readable today.

George Trask

■ **11. Thomas Moore Rhett House, c. 1820, 1009 Craven Street**. The original owner of this imposing frame house with a double piazza supported by Doric columns is unknown. It resembles the Milton Maxcy house up the street (1113 Craven Street) because both houses were owned by Rhett brothers in the 1850s, each of whom remodelled his house in the same Greek-revival style. There were five Rhett brothers, Thomas being the eldest. They were born with the last name Smith, but changed their name to Rhett in honor of their great-great-grandfather, Colonel William Rhett, whose surname had died out.

Thomas Moore Rhett (1794-1860) led a relatively quite life, unlike his politician brothers Robert and Edmund, who plotted secession at Edmund's house (1113 Craven Street). Thomas enjoyed a plantation on the Ashepoo River when not in residence here with his wife, Caroline Barnwell. He had the good sense to die four months before the beginning of the war his brothers started.

In the 20th century this house has seen a variety of uses, some of which were commercial. Members of the Tucker family operated it for decades as an inn, first as the Tucker Inn, later as the Cherokee Inn. It is now a prestigious and expensive bed and breakfast inn called the Rhett House Inn, featured in all the better travel magazines.

George Trask

HERRENHAUS AUS DER ZEIT VOR DEM BÜRGERKRIEG, BEAUFORT · IM STAAT SOUTH CAROLINA

REISEN SIE IN EINE NEUE WELT

BESUCHEN SIE DIE USA

■ **12. Joseph Johnson House,** *The Castle,* **c. 1850, 411 Craven Street.** One of the most photographed houses in America, this large mansion surrounded by an ancient garden was featured on travel posters throughout the world under President John F. Kennedy's "Visit the USA" program in the early 1960s. Massive live oaks guard the front and rear entrances, behind which stands a solid-brick facade covered with stucco, eerily like an ancient English castle. The porches overlook a strikingly handsome bend in the river, scarcely visible from the street.

Dr. Joseph Johnson, an accomplished horticulturist and an obviously wealthy man, planted the original gardens, which included olive trees imported from the Holy Land. Among his various enterprises was a brickyard on Lady's Island, enabling him to construct even the interior walls of this house of solid brick. During the Civil War Dr. Johnson's house became a hospital for wounded Federal soldiers, an outbuilding serving as a morgue. Thereafter it reverted to a private residence, lovingly cared for during most of the 20th century by the Danner family, who were collateral descendants of Dr. Johnson.

The Danners annually held a Christmas party here for almost the entire populous of the town. Howard Danner, the owner of the house, was a local merchant and an avid stamp collector, a hobby he shared with the youth of the town. After retirement from active business, he saved the John Mark Verdier house (801 Bay Street) from destruction and was a moving force in the founding of Historic Beaufort Foundation.

The Castle remains today a private home, a reminder of the grandeur of Beaufort on the eve of the Civil War.

■ **13. Henry Farmer House, c. 1810, 412 East Street.** A high tabby foundation, a stately pedimented portico, and a fine interior with extensive wainscoting and delicate staircase characterize this typical "Beaufort-style" frame house. A widow, Charlotte Beaden, acquired the house from its builder, Henry Farmer. In 1831 she married Richard Fuller (see page 73). In the same year a profound religious conversion swept the coastal South, leading Fuller to renounce his law practice and become a Baptist minister. In 1836 he toured Italy, taking time to have his portrait painted by Cavaleri, an eminent artist in Rome, and

True to the "Beaufort style", Henry Farmer built his house to face south, instead of toward the street, in order to catch the sea breezes.

bringing home seedlings of Roman laurel, which today still grow as a hedge in the garden.

■ **14. William Fripp House,** *Tidewater,* **c. 1830, 302 Fripp Street.** Beaufort's mansions tended to be built either soon after the Revolutionary War or soon before the Civil War, two periods of bountiful prosperity for Sea Island planters. This one, a well-proportioned frame structure facing south on the water, appeared in between those two wars, in about 1830. It was constructed by one of the most wealthy planters of his day, "Good Billy" Fripp, a man still remembered for his generosity and goodness. He served as a justice of the peace and a commissioner of free schools. Plantations owned by the Fripp family blanketed St. Helena Island in the decades before the Civil War. His descendants from Atlanta and other places far and wide still look upon Beaufort as their ancestral home. You may walk down the unpaved portion of Pinckney Street, on the side of this house, all the way to the water.

■ **15. Paul Hamilton House,** *The Oaks,* **c. 1856, 100 Laurens Street.** Large oaks surround the grand verandahs of this Victorian-style mansion on the Green. Built by the grandson and namesake of President James Madison's Secretary of the Navy, it was sold for Federal taxes immediately after the Civil War but redeemed by George Holmes, an honorable New Englander who became an entrepreneur here, and presented back to the Hamilton family. The house sports a roof walk, an unusual structure in Beaufort similar to ones found on mansions on Nantucket Island, Massachusetts. Its floor-to-ceiling windows and its two broad front parlors face the water to the south in the true "Beaufort style." A grassy extension of King Street runs in front of the house, allowing visitors to view its facade and the water.

George Trask

■ **16. James Robert Verdier House,** *Marshlands*, **c. 1814, 501 Pinckney Street.** This Caribbean-style mansion, with massive oaks embracing its one-story porch around three sides, symbolizes life on the Point in antebellum Beaufort. The son of John Mark Verdier (see page 75), who was a medical doctor and distinguished himself by his successful treatments against the scourge of yellow fever, built the house in 1814. Located at the end of Federal Street, it shows its western end to visitors approaching by land. Out front, facing due south, is its true beauty, a double entrance staircase to the gracious front porch, welcoming guests who might arrive by water in the old days.

When the Yankee troops arrived and ran all the white folks off the Point in 1861, the U.S. Sanitary Commission, headed by Frederick Law Olmsted, seized Verdier's mansion as its headquarters. The commission provided social services for the Union troops stationed in Beaufort throughout the war. Olmsted, a New Englander and the landscape-architect genius who created Central Park in New York City, travelled in the early 1850s by steamboat, railroad, stagecoach, and horseback through Virginia, the Carolinas, Georgia, Alabama, and Louisiana. As he went, he wrote a series of newspaper articles for the *New-York Daily Times* (now known as *The New York Times*), which he later compiled into an immensely popular book, still in print after 140 years, entitled *The Cotton Kingdom*. If you really want to know what the South was like before the Civil War, you must read Olmsted's book.

The other side of the story, about a family of ultra-rich planters in Beaufort, was told by Frances Griswold in his fictionalized account entitled *A Sea Island Lady*. The couple who owned this house in the 1940s liked Griswold's story so much that they attached the name "Marshlands," Griswold's invention, to their house. Actually, Griswold was describing "Tabby Manse," the old Fuller mansion on Bay Street in which he stayed while writing the book in the late 1930s.

George Trask

■ **17. Berners Barnwell Sams House No. 2, 1852, 201 Laurens Street.** B.B. Sams built this serene brick classical-revival mansion in 1852, 34 years after the first house he built at 310 New Street. Taking a cue from his own name, he and his wife bestowed lyrical alliterations on all fifteen of their children: William Washington, Donald Decatur, Ariana Adelaide, etc. Poetry was a powerful force in the house even after the Civil War, when the Reverend A.P. Hay, the "poet of the Confederacy," lived here.

B.B.'s brother, Lewis Reeve, built his mansion at 601 Bay Street in the same year this house was built, 1852. The Sams brothers owned more than 3,500 acres on Lady's and Datha Islands. They spent most of the year on their Datha Island lands, coming to town in summer to enjoy their mansions. The venerable Datha name, brought down from time immemorial by the indigenous Indians, has recently (and temporarily we trust) been bastardized to Dataw by real estate marketers.

Facing the Green, this house is unusual in Beaufort for its remaining complete set of dependencies along the rear, which housed a blacksmith shop, a cookhouse, a laundry, a storeroom, and servants' quarters in the era of King Cotton. Surrounding the enclave is a masonry wall with a stone slab on the street to help ladies and gentlemen into their carriages (see photograph on page 42).

■ **18. The Green** is a private park in front of the B. B. Sams house, totally open with massive oaks on its boundaries, encompassing an entire city block, helping to make old Beaufort an especially wonderful place. Imagine, if you will, what Gramercy Park in New York City or Place des Vosges in Paris would be like without a locked fence and the tribulations of a large city today. That's the Green.

■ **19. Edgar Fripp House,** *Tidalholm,* **c. 1856, 1 Laurens Street.** At the tip of the Point, surrounded by a locked gate to maintain privacy and by water on three sides, stands this frame house with its special aura. "Proud Edgar" Fripp built it as his summer house just a few years after his neighbor and fellow island planter, B.B. Sams, built a brick mansion in the adjoining block. After the Civil Way the Fripp family regained possession when a generous Frenchman bought the house at the Federal auction and, in a gesture of supreme generosity, presented the deed to the Fripps. More recently Tidalholm was the principal setting for the filming of two blockbuster movies, *The Great Santini* and *The Big Chill.* Originally Italianate in design with a one-story verandah, this grand house was modified into the "Beaufort style" after the 1893 hurricane blew off the roof and the second story.

George Trask

■ **20. Elizabeth Hext House,** *Riverview*, **c. 1720, 207 Hancock Street.** When this house was built, its location put it out in the countryside away from the tiny town. A small, intimate structure on a large lot, it remains a country cottage, far removed in style from the numerous grand mansions that in the next century became its neighbors on the Point. Its owners, Elizabeth Hext (1746-1813) and her husband, William Sams (died 1793), were responsible for two of the mansions. It was they who purchased Datha Island in 1786, began growing cotton there, and bequeathed it to their two sons, B.B. and Lewis Reeve Sams. The sons made fortunes from the cotton and built two of the largest summer mansions on the Point in the 1850s. In such ways as these, almost all of the old houses in Beaufort are related. Elizabeth Hext's husband, William Sams, was descended from "Tuscarora Jack" Barnwell. His Barnwell and Fuller cousins built the great mansions on Bay Street.

George Trask

■ **21. The Reverend Thomas E. Ledbetter House, c. 1840, 411 Bayard Street.** Situated on the largest residential lot in old Beaufort, this typical "Beaufort style" house proves the rule—it faces south to catch the summer breeze and the winter sun even though the water lies at its back door. Its builder was a Methodist minister who came to Beaufort to evangelize the slaves on the islands. After the Civil War Niels Christensen, Sr., a Dane who fought for the Union and who became superintendent of the National Cemetery here, bought the house. His wife, Abbie Holmes Christensen, founded one of the first Montessori schools in the South in this house in 1917. One of their friends, Clara Barton, founder of American Red Cross, visited them in Beaufort after the 1893 hurricane.

The Reverend Ledbetter's house in the days of the ox and cart, a means of hauling in Beaufort as late as the 1950s.

■ **22. Elizabeth Barnwell Gough House, c. 1789, 705 Washington Street.** Another of the many mansions of the Barnwell family, this solid tabby one is almost an identical twin of "Tabby Manse" (1211 Bay Street) with minor differences in the portico and in the floor plan. Elizabeth Barnwell (1753-1817) through her unhappy marriage to Captain Richard Gough (1750-1796) produced a daughter, Mariana. Mariana produced ten children, one of whom was Robert Barnwell Rhett, the "father of Secession" (see page 90). After enduring the indignity of having its interior panelling removed in the 1930s and becoming a boarding house, this mansion has in recent years been brought back to life in all its glory as a private residence.

George Trask

George Trask

Other Major Points of Interest

■ **U.S. Marine Corps Recruit Depot Parris Island**, five miles south of downtown Beaufort, sits in view of town as you stand looking south from the high bluff on Bay Street. To reach Parris Island, take Bay Street onto Ribaut Road and follow the signs south to the Parris Island gate.

This depot began as a U.S. Navy station with a small detachment of Marines in 1891. It has grown to become the main recruit training station for the United States Marine Corps, more than one million men and women having gone through basic training here since 1915. Almost the entire depot is open to the public. Facilities include a post exchange, a commissary, a fitness center, a golf course, a library, and a military museum. Today, as many as 29,000 recruits a year graduate to become Marines in awe-inspiring ceremonies each Friday morning. Sword drills and parade marches performed to perfection, with stirring music by the Marine Corps Band, make up the 90-minute ceremony. Guaranteed to rekindle patriotic fires. Call the Douglas Visitors' Center on the base for more information.

The Parris Island depot is located on historic ground indeed. French Huguenots landed here in 1562, and the Spanish built the fort of Santa Elena four years later. These sites can be reached by car and observed up close on foot. Several archaeological digs have been performed here, as well as performances of reenactments of the French and Spanish landings. Be sure to check in April or May if the dig is going on; the archaeologists enjoy giving tours. If you have the time and the inclination, you can help them dig. Also of note on Parris Island is the inspirational Iwo Jima Monument (see photo opposite), located near the parade deck, which was the original prototype for the more renowned monument erected later in Washington, D.C.

■ **Parris Island Museum** is a source of information not only for the depot, but for general military history as well. The museum is spit-polished, as you might expect. Exhibits cover the span of Marine Corps history. Plan to spend a good bit of time here if you are a military buff.

■ **U.S. Naval Hospital Beaufort** is located on Ribaut Road, midway between downtown Beaufort and the Parris Island gate. Originally a tiny infirmary located on Parris Island, the medical facility flourished there during World Wars I and II, reaching 800 patients a day during the 1940s when hundreds of thousands of recruits underwent training for wartime duty. In 1949 construction was completed on the present-day hospital, relocated off the island on a beautiful oak-covered site along the Beaufort River which includes the ruins of the ancient Fort Frederick and the grounds of the Civil War Camp Saxton. Today the hospital, with a potential capacity of 246 beds, serves not only military personnel stationed at Parris Island and the Air Station, but also military families living elsewhere in nearby areas of South Carolina and Georgia.

■ **U.S. National Cemetery**, intersection of Bladen and Boundary Streets, just outside the downtown historic district, dates back to 1863 when it was established as one of twelve national cemeteries by President Abraham Lincoln. Most of those buried here are Union soldiers from the Civil War. This is a tranquil place with massive old live oaks and magnolia trees. Each year on Memorial Day (called Decoration Day here), the graves are decorated and a memorial service is held in memory of the war dead of our nation.

■ **U.S. Marine Corps Air Station Beaufort** began in 1954 on the grounds of a deactivated World-War-II naval air station, five miles north of Beaufort. The government purchased numerous tracts of farmland to expand the facility to cover almost 7,000 acres, the first permanent air station built exclusively for Marine aviation. The current officers' club stands in the midst of a pecan grove on what was once a major truck farm. Former vegetable fields now covered with concrete and asphalt create the longest military runway east of the Mississippi River (12,200 feet), earning this airport the designation as an alternate landing site for the space shuttle. Beginning with Korean War fighter jets, the complement of warplanes at the air station has evolved through numerous generations: FJ-3 Furies, F-8 Crusaders, A-4 Skyhawks, F-4 Phantom IIs, and now F/A-18 Hornets. The air station is home to Marine Aircraft Group-31, whose combat exploits include air action in the Iraqi campaign in 1991. Families reside at the nearby Laurel Bay military housing complex of 1,100 homes.

George Trask

■ **Old Sheldon Church Ruins**, about a half-hour's drive from downtown Beaufort, are all that remain of Prince William's Parish Church, built 1745-55. British troops burned the original structure during the Revolutionary War. Reconstructed in 1825, the edifice was torched again by General Sherman's troops in their march across South Carolina in early 1865. Conceived as a Greek temple, the structure is considered to be one of the first in the Greek-revival style in America. Outside its walls, behind the altar, are the marble tombs of members of the Bull family, who owned vast tracts of land in this area before the Civil War. The congregation of St. Helena's Episcopal Church holds an outdoor service here once a year on the second Sunday after Easter, public invited. Take Highway 21 north to the intersection with Highway 17, bear left, go about 500 yards, turn right onto Secondary Road 21, and follow the signs to Sheldon Church.

George Trask

■ **Chapel of Ease**, on Lands End Road on St. Helena Island, is located about a mile past the Penn Center campus. The remains of this church, built of tabby and brick, still stand today following damage by fire in 1886. The church was built in 1740 to serve planters living on the outlying Sea Islands, thus the name Chapel of Ease for its convenient location.

■ **Fort Fremont**, at Lands End on St. Helena Island, was built during the Spanish-American War to guard the entrance to Port Royal Sound. Remains of the hospital building and concrete gun emplacements still stand, but beware of ghosts. A very famous ghost, who is rumored to be a soldier who lost his head, is said to lurk here at night. The ghost carries a lantern, which appears as a mysterious light, as he searches the grounds for his head. Go several miles past Penn Center and the Chapel of Ease to the end of Lands End Road.

■ **Penn Center**, St. Helena Island, was established in 1862 by Quakers from Philadelphia. Penn Normal School became world renowned as the first school in the South for freed slaves following emancipation. When the public school system took over primary and secondary education in the first half of the 20th century, the school became an interracial conference center, training center, and retreat. Recent renovations have brought the campus buildings back to pristine condition. There is a museum of black history with artifacts, sweetgrass baskets, weavings, historical books, and photographs of students from Penn Normal School. The late Dr. Martin Luther King, Jr., used this campus as a retreat to plan his famous March On Washington. Go across the downtown bridge straight ahead on Highway 21 south to Frogmore on St. Helena Island, then turn right onto Martin Luther King Drive and go about a mile.

The New Bell

I had expressed a wish for a bell for my school-house, hoping to bring about a more regular attendance, with less delay. Immediately a Boston friend, who had been in the department, responded by sending me just what I needed. Oh, what a delight was this bell to the whole neighborhood! The children would collect around the house very early, and lie on the ground waiting and watching for it to ring. For a long time this was a mystery incomprehensible to them. They talked often to each other about "we bell," and seemed to feel as if each one had a kind of right of possession in it.

"Oh, but him can talk loud!" said the boys with delight. I told them all what the bell was for, where it came from, and who sent it. Without consulting me they immediately named the school for our generous friend, "Hooper School, A No. 1."

The children were allowed to take turns in ringing the bell; but this was a privilege only granted as a reward for good behavior.

—Elizabeth Hyde Botume, *First Days Amongst the Contrabands*, 1893

Rudolf Eickemeyer, courtesy of John Lyon

Well-behaved grandchildren of the contrabands ringing the school bell on St. Helena Island about 1920.

Hunting Island lighthouse in its heyday as a beacon for ships, before the keeper's house disappeared.

■ **Hunting Island State Park**, is a public beach and ocean-front park about a twenty-minute drive from downtown Beaufort, south on Highway 21. Miles of beaches, unusually wide at low tide, beckon you for walking, sunning, running, and generally playing. Shell collecting is a favorite pastime here; however, please take only empty shells and dead sand dollars so future generations can enjoy this pastime too. Small waves and shallow water make Hunting Island an ideal outing for children. Rest rooms and vending facilities are available, though no lifeguards are present. There are also nature trails winding through the subtropical landscape. The plant life in this park is unusually dramatic: tall pines, palmettos, and draping oak. Check with the Hunting Island Visitors' Center (follow signs at entrance to park) for trail information. A marshfront boardwalk on the side of Hunting Island opposite the ocean is part of the park. This is a nature walk literally through the marsh. Be sure to look in the marsh carefully for crabs and birds—there is teeming life here.

■ **Hunting Island Lighthouse**. an active lighthouse until 1933, is open to the public to enjoy spectacular views from the top. Take a left at the signs to the north beach at Hunting Island; it's a long and twisty road. First established in 1859, the lighthouse was relocated in 1860 due to beach erosion. In 1889 it had to be moved again.

. . . the golden Bass; and the Drum, with its mysterious, and, to a stranger, its startling sound; and the Porpoise, showing its back above the water; and the unseen and unsuspected tribes, that thronged the depths below; the Sting-ray, with its jagged spine; the Saw-fish; the omnivorous Shark; and mightiest, strangest, most formidable among them all for its strength—the Devil-fish. Whoever has seen the beautiful bay on which they are seated (known on the map as Port Royal Sound), with its transparent waters stocked with a variety of sea-fish, while the islands that gird it abound in deer and other game—will confess that it is a position well calculated to draw out whatever sporting propensities may have been implanted in us by nature.

—William Elliott, *Carolina Sports by Land and Water*, 1846

George Trask

Flora & Fauna of the Sea Islands

■ **Alligator.** Depending on your curiosity and fortitude, you may or may not want to encounter this reptile. Alligators live in our freshwater ponds, not in the ocean or the saltwater creeks. They can grow up to 15 feet in length, weighing 500 pounds. Smaller than crocodiles (which are found in Africa, not here), they can be distinguished by wide, flat snouts. In winter they hibernate in underground dens, appearing again in March. You can safely observe them from the bridge over the pond at Hunting Island State Park, though you may have to search the water carefully, for they are masters of disguise. Respect this fascinating reptile; *never* try to feed one. It will charge and can outrun you for 50 yards. If you find yourself in this most unfortunate predicament, retreat rapidly in a zigzag pattern; alligators have trouble turning quickly while running. Errant golfer's tip: don't try to save money by retrieving your ball out of a pond unless you want to become an alligator's dinner. And be careful if you have a dog. 'Gators eat dogs for hors d'oeuvres.

■ **Azalea.** Spring hasn't totally sprung in Beaufort until the azaleas come into bloom in late March or early April. The brilliant flowers on these shrubs come in colors of white, pink, orchid, salmon, and crimson. They can be found in just about everyone's garden here. The traditional *indica* varieties are the ones with large and abundant blossoms. The most popular ones in the Beaufort area are Gerbing (white), George Tabor (blush pink), Pride of Mobile (pink), Judge Solomon (deep pink), Pride of Summerville (orchid), and Formosa (deep orchid).

■ **Centipede Grass.** Newcomers to Beaufort from other climes often assume that they can plant the same varieties of grass in their front yards as they mowed back home on Long Island or in Cleveland. Not so. Lawn grasses of colder climates wither and die under the humid and blistering summer sun here. There is only one variety that is guaranteed to satisfy: centipede, a summer grass that spreads from stolons. Somewhat difficult to establish by seeding, it makes an instant lawn if installed as sod, which is readily available locally. Centipede loves full sun, tolerates moderate shade, withstands moderate drought, chokes out weeds, dislikes fertilizer, and hates close mowing. And it looks good too. Now that's a perfect grass. Knowledgeable Beaufortonians treasure the color of centipede in winter, which matches the incomparable cordgrass that grows along the rivers and creeks. They would never commit the unnatural act of overseeding it with winter ryegrass to camouflage the glorious golden color of centipede in winter.

■ **Cordgrass or Spartina.** This is the dominant tall grass of the marsh, growing to six feet in height. Cordgrass bakes in the mud at temperatures up to 140 degrees at low tide, then endures inundation by salt water as the tide rises, all the while looking like a robust field of wheat waving in the breeze, green in summer, golden in winter. Thousands upon thousands of acres of nature's fields of marshgrass surround the Sea Islands, harboring sealife and birdlife of all kinds.

■ **Blue Crab.** A delicacy in the South, blue crabs thrive in our tidal waterways and appear on most of the menus in our local restaurants. Those floating bottles and balls you see in the waterways mark crab traps made of wire mesh. Don't rob the traps. They are somebody's livelihood, and local fishermen guard them with ferocity. Instead, get a chicken neck, tie it to a string, and throw it into the water off any dock. When you feel a tug, pull slowly; up will come a crab. Keep only crabs that are five inches or larger across the shell. Throw the smaller ones back into the water as well as all females with eggs—it's the law.

■ **Fiddler Crab.** These crabs are too small for eating, but they sure can fiddle. Look for them among the dead cordgrass that washes ashore along tidal flats at low tide. You'll recognize them immediately with their single, oversized claw (male only), which they use as a weapon and for feeding. They also use their "fiddle" for courting females—just a wave and the girls come running. Fiddler crabs make good fish bait, especially if you're casting for sheepshead.

■ **Sand Crab or Ghost Crab.** These little crabs live in sand holes on the dry part of the beach. They're so swift that you're likely to observe them closely only after dark when you can shine a flashlight in their eyes. Beige in color, they blend with the sand, hence their name since they seem to vanish before your very eyes. The name may also come from the fact that they move so quickly that it's a case of "now you see them, now you don't."

A lazy Sunday afternoon in the Sea Islands: industrious boy lifts trap full of blue crabs out of creek, just in time for supper.

■ **Loggerhead Sea Turtle.** Count yourself lucky should you see a loggerhead turtle. These creatures face harrowing circumstances in the cycle of life. Between May and August females drag their 350-pound bodies up the beach at an excruciatingly slow pace. They dig a nest for hours with their giant flippers to lay about 150 eggs. They spend more hours kicking sand over the nest, then drag themselves back down the beach to the sea. Two months later, if the nest has been undisturbed by raccoons, crabs and people, hatchlings emerge and scamper to the beach, vulnerable to preying birds. Once in the ocean, the young turtles face fish whose favorite dish is turtle soup. Virtually 99.9 % of the young don't make it to adulthood. The ones that do are rewarded with lives of 100 years or more. If you spot a loggerhead nest, *do not* disturb it, but report its location immediately to the park ranger or the local turtle protection project. Never shine a light on loggerhead turtles, and keep lights around beach houses to a minimum. Help us protect our precious turtles.

The Fish-Hawk

Aloft the fish-hawk wings his wary way,
Stops, turns, and watches the incautious prey,
Quick as the fish attracts his piercing eye,
With fluttered wings a moment poised on high,
Headlong he plunges with unerring aim,
In iron claws secures the struggling game,
Upward again his joyous flight resumes,
And shakes the water from his ruffled plumes.

—William J. Grayson, Beaufort, S.C., 1854

■ **Magnolia.** You can find magnolias everywhere here, steel and otherwise. The ones of which we are most fond are trees that grow to a height of 80 feet, have large, dark green leathery leaves, and from summer into fall produce the most robust flowers (8-10 inches across) you ever laid your eyes on. The association between the South and magnolias is so strong that it's difficult to pronounce magnolia without a drawl.

■ **Osprey or Fish-Hawk.** The words "regal" and "majestic" describe this powerful bird of prey. Often mistaken for an eagle, osprey can be distinguished by white feathers dominating underneath with brown feathers topside on wings and back. When they fly their bent-shaped wings span five feet. Osprey fish for a living, swooping down feet first and using their gigantic talons to snatch fish literally out of the water. They like to build nests close by tidal waters on power poles, bridge-tender roofs, channel markers, and buoys. Osprey mate for life. Human animals sometimes install tall poles near waterways in hopes of attracting a pair to nest.

■ **Porpoise or Bottle-nosed Dolphin.** Most folks think these playful mammals inhabit only ocean waters, but porpoises love to cruise our inshore tidal waterways too. Highly social animals, they are usually found in small schools of four to six. You may see them around fishing boats, either playfully swimming alongside, or hoping for a free bite or two. Also look for them at the beach, surfing the ocean waves. A famous albino porpoise was captured in Beaufort waters some years ago and taken to a Florida aquarium. As a result, the South Carolina state legislature has outlawed the capture of porpoises for aquatic display.

■ **Sand Dollar.** Though rarely thought of as animals, sand dollars are living, breathing creatures. The five petals you see embossed on their faces are used for filtration and breathing. The center of the flower is a water sucking device providing power for hundreds of tiny tube feet on their undersides. The tube feet move sand dollars around and carry food to their mouths. The mouth, at the center of the underside, has tiny teeth for straining and chewing. Shell seekers must take only sand dollars that are dead (white or brown). If they are still greenish and alive, be sure to return them to deeper water.

■ **Sea Oats.** The tall grass that grows along the dunes of our beaches is a close relative of the grain we grow to eat, but in this case the grain grows wild and provides protection from beach erosion. If you fancy taking some home to display in a vase in your living room, be forewarned: these plants are so valuable to our beach ecology that it is illegal to cut or pick them, and you could go to jail.

■ **Wading Birds.** At our beaches you will see hordes of birds wading in the foam or flying above the waves—black skimmers, brown pelicans, oystercatchers, ruddy turnstones, and all kinds of gulls and terns. The marsh is where you will see the bird that defines our Sea Islands perhaps better than any other—the great egret, a statuesque white bird that has become an icon of the Lowcountry. Once hunted to the edge of extinction for their prized plumes, egrets now flourish here thanks to past efforts of the Audubon Society. The great egret is three to four feet tall, with white plumage, black legs, and a long, yellow bill. When you see a smaller white bird in the marsh with long plumes, that's a snowy egret. Keep on the lookout for another dazzling marsh bird, the great blue heron. Though four feet tall, this bird is harder to spot because its plumes are a blue and gray color that blends into the environment. Stunning.

Hollywood Comes to Beaufort

MORE THAN A DOZEN major motion pictures have been filmed in Beaufort, bringing an unexpected fame to the town. In addition to telling compelling stories, famous films express the popularity of certain dramatic themes and the popularity of certain movie stars. The themes covered in the films made in Beaufort have almost all been emotionally sensitive and uplifting. The actors have included some of the best known and most highly respected names in American film making.

A Beaufort author, Pat Conroy, is primarily responsible for this beneficent state of affairs. When it was announced in the late 1970s that his first sensationally popular novel, *The Great Santini*, was going to be made into a movie in Beaufort, no one could foresee the impact movie making would have on the town. But when the stars arrived—Robert Duvall and Blythe Danner—and they immediately fell in love with Beaufort, there was an inkling of what was to come. Not only did the film introduce Beaufort to the millions of people who saw it, it also revealed Beaufort to film makers as a perfect location to portray many different moments in time. The carefully preserved old houses in the historic district, spanning almost three centuries, looked as they did when originally built. The thriving downtown business district, several generations removed in appearance from the suburban shopping malls of today, looked as it did in the 1940s and 1950s. And the massive live oak trees, the verdant salt marshes, and the wide expanses of open water portrayed the majesty and beauty of eternal nature.

The result for Beaufort has been a parade of major motion pictures and a parade of major stars. Casting calls have brought long lines of normally unassertive Beaufortonians, hoping for a shot at celluloid fame, shoulder to shoulder with some of Hollywood's biggest names. Scores of residents have been extras, and Beaufortonians have had speaking parts in some of the most celebrated films the world has ever seen. Beaufort has become big box office in the States and abroad, the films made here grossing hundreds of millions of dollars for the film industry and making the little town of Beaufort, previously a byway, known almost everywhere. Listed below are the major films that have been made here:

■ **Gullah Gullah Island**. Film making has brought celebrity status to Beaufort natives Ron and Natalie Daise, stars of *Gullah Gullah Island*, the Emmy-nominated children's television program featured on Nickelodean. You can see a lot of the Gullah influence on the Sea Islands in this delightful show, which is filled with great songs, stories, and enchanting characters. Some episodes are filmed in beautiful downtown Beaufort, with local children getting into the act as location extras.

■ **Conrack** (1974). A perennial favorite on trans-Atlantic air flights and late-night re-runs, *Conrack* was the first nationally-distributed film made about the Beaufort area. It was adapted from *The Water Is Wide,* an early novel by local author Pat Conroy—the first of his novels to gain national recognition. Although this movie was actually filmed on the coast in nearby Georgia, it is about Conroy's experiences and struggles as a lonely elementary public school teacher in an isolated black community on Daufuskie Island in Beaufort county. When the county school board fired Conroy after he took the children on an unauthorized school trip off the island, a classic confrontation ensued between the idealistic young teacher and the local educational bureaucracy. Jon Voight portrayed Conroy in the leading role in this film.

■ **The Great Santini** (1980). Starring Robert Duvall and Blythe Danner, this is the story of a dysfunctional military family headed by a stern, mercurial fighter-jet pilot. It was based on the novel of the same name written by Beaufort's own Pat Conroy, who grew up on the Point in Beaufort's historic district. Conroy wrote this novel about his real-life father, stationed at the U.S. Marine Corps Air Station Beaufort, with whom he had a struggling personal relationship. Duvall's co-star, Tony-award-winning actress Blythe Danner, brought her daughter Gwyneth Paltrow, a young child at the time and now a famous actress in her own right, on location with her. In contrast to Conroy, Paltrow has been quoted as saying that her time in Beaufort was one of the happiest and most pleasant of her childhood. Duvall, who showed his tennis prowess in games with the locals on the city courts, loved Beaufort so

Pat Conroy grew up among U.S. Marines stationed at Parris Island and the Air Station.

much that he served as grand marshal in Beaufort's Water Festival parade. In 1995 he came back to star in *Something to Talk About* with Julia Roberts. The majestic home on the Point known as Tidalholm, later used as the setting for *The Big Chill*, was first featured in this film.

■ **The Big Chill** (1983). Recipient of four Academy-award nominations, this production featured a memorable collection of upbeat Motown songs and some of the biggest stars of our time, including Tom Berenger, William Hurt, Glenn Close, Jeff Goldblum, JoBeth Williams, Kevin Kline, Mary Kay Place, and Meg Tilly. The mansion known as Tidalholm on the Point was the setting for this 30-something tale, a cult film to baby-boomers, of old college chums who reunite after many years when one of their classmates dies. Such fame came to Tidalholm because of this film that it is now known to out-of-towners as "The Big Chill House." Some indoor

Courtesy of Ned Brown

Bay Street in the 1950s, decades before William Hurt and Kevin Kline jogged this street in The Big Chill.

scenes were filmed on sets built inside the National Guard Armory on Rogers Street. Cast members got a firsthand taste of the easy life in Beaufort while filming this movie. Tom Berenger loved the lifestyle so much that he made Beaufort his permanent home.

■ **Charlotte Forten's Mission: Experiment in Freedom** (1985). American Playhouse produced this film for the Public Broadcasting System, the true story of Charlotte Forten, a well-educated and wealthy black Philadelphia missionary who traveled to St. Helena Island in 1862 to help educate the newly freed slaves. Her diary has become one of the major historical resources about the role of women during the Civil War. Noteworthy Beaufortonians had speaking parts, performing better (in the opinion of their spouses) than many of the professionals. There are gorgeous scenes in this film of the islands and waterways surrounding Beaufort.

■ **Glory** (1989). Denzel Washington and Morgan Freeman gave masterful performances in this awe-inspiring but graphically violent war film about the Massachusetts 54th Regiment, America's most famous unit of black soldiers during the Civil War. The film, which garnered nine Academy Award nominations, won three Oscars. The 54th Regiment, under the command of Colonel Robert Shaw, was quartered in Beaufort during the Civil War and left here on its bloody rendezvous with destiny at Fort Wagner near Charleston. The battered remnants of the regiment, many soldiers terribly wounded, returned to Beaufort. Many of those who died lie under the shade of the oaks, magnolias, and palmettos in the National Cemetery on Boundary Street. Augustus Saint-Gaudens' heroic bronze statue in Boston Commons, directly in front of the Massachusetts State House, commemorates the gallantry of the Massachusetts 54th. Parts of the film were shot in the rural areas surrounding Beaufort, which have remained much the same as they looked during the Civil War. The Public Broadcasting System subsequently filmed a documentary production here on the same subject, aired under the title *The Massachusetts 54th*.

■ **The Prince of Tides** (1991). An adaptation of another exceptionally popular Pat Conroy novel set in his hometown of Beaufort, this movie received nine Oscar nominations including Best Actor (Nick Nolte) and Best Picture. Barbara Streisand, the principal actress and the director, became a temporary local during the filming. She lived in a house on the Point and, pursuing her passion for art, became a regular at the Rhett Gallery on Bay Street. Her co-star, Nick Nolte, also took a house on the Point, and toured Beaufort Bay on sunset cruises. The enchanting Blythe Danner, who was the charm

The tides of which every boy was a prince in the days when Beaufort was an unknown byway.

of Beaufort during the filming of *The Great Santini*, returned to star in this film as Nolte's wife. Kate Nelligan, Melinda Dillon, and George Carlin completed the named cast. Vast expanses of Beaufort's natural scenery, so lyrically described by Conroy in the novel, enhance the film.

■ **Daughters of the Dust** (1992) This underground classic, subsequently released in selected theaters across the nation, caused a sensation among followers of non-Hollywood film making. Directed by award-winning cinematographer Julie Dash, it portrays the struggles of a strong, matriarchal Gullah family grappling with an age-old dilemma: whether to remain together in their rural paradise on an island or seek their fortunes in modernity on the mainland.

■ **Forrest Gump** (1994). More than any other film, this movie about a lovable, slightly retarded good old boy who accomplishes great things has contributed to the continuing popularity of Beaufort as a film-making location. Winner of *nine* Oscars including Best Picture, this critically acclaimed film includes an emotional, Oscar-winning performance by Tom Hanks. Containing camera wizardry never before seen on the silver screen, the film also garnered an Oscar for special effects. During the filming, cast members including Sally Field, Robin Wright, and Gary Sinise frequented area shops and restaurants, leaving locals star-struck. Boombears, Beaufort's famous toy emporium, was especially popular with cast members accompanied by their children. Visitors to Beaufort continue to enjoy the ambiance depicted in this film by dining at the 11th Street Dockside restaurant in Port Royal, which offers front-row viewing of the boats and docks featured in the "Bubba Gump Shrimp Company" scenes.

■ **The War** (1994). Kevin Costner and Elijah Wood starred in this intense and poignant portrait of a troubled Vietnam War veteran, his son, and their small town life. The angel oak tree depicted in the tree-house scene, a favorite climbing spot for local kids, is located at Grady's Point on the outskirts of Beaufort.

■ **Rudyard Kipling's The Jungle Book** (1994). Lions and tigers and bears were not the only stars of this Disney fantasy-adventure filmed mostly on Beaufort's lush, tropical Fripp Island. Jason Scott Lee, John Cleese, and Sam Neill were featured in this live-action adaptation of Kipling's *Mowgli* stories about an orphaned boy in India who leads an assorted crew of children and rogues to a magical jungle city.

George Trask

"Miss St. Helena" at the shrimp dock at Port Royal in 1957, before Buppa Gump was a gleam in anybody's eye.

■ **Something to Talk About** (1995). Julia Roberts starred with Dennis Quaid and supporting players Gena Rowlands, Kyra Sedgwick, and Robert Duvall in this comic farce about marital turmoil. In their off time on location in Beaufort, the stars enjoyed the best of the town. Julia Roberts was in evidence at frequent elegant dinners with friends while she stayed at the Beaufort Inn. Kyra Sedgwick strolled Bay Street with husband Kevin Bacon, Robert Duvall fished with local Orvis guides, and director Lasse Hallstrom golfed at local courses.

■ **White Squall** (1996). Jeff Bridges starred in this Ridley Scott-directed film of young men bound for disaster on the high seas. Set in the early 1960s and based on a true story, this suspenseful production depicted students sailing a brigantine in pristine Caribbean waters (actually, the waters surrounding Beaufort) who encounter a life-threatening storm. The cast included Caroline Goodall, John Savage, Scott Wolf, Jeremy Sisto, Ryan Phillippe, and David Lascher.

■ **Last Dance** (1996). Sharon Stone's arrival in Beaufort for the filming of this movie created the typical stir. Stone played a death row inmate in this commentary on capital punishment. Rob Morrow played her attorney, while Randy Quaid and Peter Gallagher rounded out the cast. Stone's gritty performance drew attention to the drama of prison existence.

■ **G.I. Jane** (1997). Demi Moore portrayed a woman soldier amidst the male domain of the U.S. military system. Moore sported a military-style crewcut and underwent intense fitness training in preparation for the film, shot mostly at the lagoon on Hunting Island. Living at "The Castle" on Craven Street during the film shoot, Moore and her daughters often strolled downtown, carrying on chance conversations with shopkeepers and newly found friends in Beaufort.

■ **Forces of Nature** (1999). Ben Affleck and Sandra Bullock are paired in this comedy romance centered around whether Affleck is or isn't going to get to the church on time. If he does he'll marry sweet Bridget (*NewsRadio's* Maura Tierney); if he doesn't he'll run off with sweet Sarah (Sandra Bullock), with whom he falls madly in love on the way to the wedding. Beaufort's adopted theatrical grande dame, Blythe Danner, plays Bridget's mother. Steve Zahn offers comic support in his role as Affleck's best friend. The real star is the weather, that force of nature portrayed as a downpour worthy of the great flood of biblical times.

■ **Rules of Engagement** (2000). Battlefield and terrorist blood and gore coupled with high drama in the courtroom bring Tommy Lee Jones and Samuel L. Jackson together as protagonists in this Marine Corps drama. Filming on Parris Island and Hunting Island add realism to settings depicting military life and Vietnam battlefield action. Ben Kingsley plays a U.S. ambassador in a Middle East hot spot that erupts into a hostage crisis and a rescue slaughterhouse. Definitely not for the high minded or the faint of heart.

Literary Beaufort

LONG BEFORE movies came to Beaufort, books were being written about the place, the first ones by European explorers who arrived here soon after Columbus discovered America. Literature inspired by the Beaufort area thus goes back almost to the beginning of printed books. These are books about Beaufort that we especially like:

■ **New World explorer.** No sooner had Jean Ribaut returned to France after his voyage here in 1562 than he sat down to write a narrative of the expedition, translated into English the next year as *The Whole and True Discoverye of Terra Florida*. Ribaut's description of Port Royal Sound as "one of the greatest and fairest havens in the world" has never been surpassed.

■ **American naturalists and outdoorsmen.** Mark Catesby, commissioned by wealthy Englishmen including the founder of the British Museum, was the first English naturalist to catalog the flora and fauna of coastal America. In the 1720s he came to the Beaufort area to study and draw the amazing diversity of plants and animals here. His masterpiece of 220 hand-colored engravings, *Natural History of Carolina, Florida and the Bahama Islands*, became the basis used by Linnaeus for his systematic cataloging of American species. A century later the French-American naturalist John James Audubon (1785-1851) came to nearby Charleston to follow in Catesby's footsteps, leaving his four-volume *The Birds of America* as the most famous series of American bird drawings. Yet another century later a man born to cotton wealth in Beaufort, William Elliott (1788-1863), wrote here *Carolina Sports by Land and Water* about Beaufort's outdoor sporting life of hunting and fishing, a book so popular that it has remained in print almost without interruption since 1846.

■ **Antebellum poet and preacher.** William J. Grayson and Richard Fuller were native sons of Beaufort in the days of aristocratic cotton wealth. Both became Beaufort lawyers, Grayson through education at South Carolina College and Fuller at Harvard College. Grayson wrote poetry, entered politics, and became a U.S. Congressman; Fuller saw the light and became a Baptist preacher. Both Grayson and Fuller in their separate roles as poet and preacher defended slavery through writings that made them famous. Grayson's epic poem *The Hireling and the Slave* (1854) argued that slaves led better lives in the agrarian South than laborers in the cotton mills of New England, a view confirmed by modern-day sociologists. Fuller argued that the Bible justified slavery in a famous debate between him and Francis Wayland, president of Rhode Island College (now called Brown University), published in 1845 as *Domestic Slavery considered as a Scriptural Institution.* Both Grayson and Fuller redeemed themselves before the Civil War, Grayson by opposing the secession of South Carolina that provoked the war and Fuller by selling his slaves, moving to Baltimore, and serving as President Lincoln's conduit for messages between the Federal government and Southern land owners.

■ **Civil War diarists.** A special literary genre with roots running deep in Beaufort soil is Civil War letters and diaries by missionaries and entrepreneurs. Their writings constitute a treasure trove of information about wartime conditions here, the human drama of the Federal occupation, and the thrill of the emancipation of the slaves. We especially commend the following, most of which are currently available in excellent paperback editions—*The Journal of Charlotte L. Forten,* a free-born, well-educated, articulate young black woman from

Philadelphia who served as a missionary to the newly freed slaves in 1862-64; the diary of Dr. Esther Hill Hawks, a woman medical doctor from New Hampshire who fought to save the lives of the wounded Federal soldiers in the churches converted into military hospitals here, titled *A Woman's Civil War* ; the memoirs of Colonel Thomas Wentworth Higginson, a Massachusetts native who attended Harvard College and Harvard Divinity School, then commanded here the First South Carolina Volunteers, the first American regular army regiment of freed slaves, titled *Army Life in a Black Regiment*; *Letters and Diary of Laura M. Towne,* the wartime missionary from Philadelphia who dedicated her life to educating at Penn School on St. Helena Island the former slaves and their children after the war ended; and *Letters from Port Royal, 1862-1868,* a series of letters sure to shatter your preconceptions written by Edward S. Philbrick, William C. Gannett, Harriet Ware, and Charles Preston Ware, Bostonians in Beaufort during the war.

■ **Civil War novelists.** Coming at the time when the generation that fought the Civil War had finally passed away, Margaret Mitchell's *Gone with the Wind* took America by storm in 1936. Distant memories of the war became romance between fiery Scarlett O'Hara and dashing Rhett Butler. Competing large publishing companies raced to release a knock-off version to cannibalize on the novel's popularity. Nelson Doubleday, who owned a plantation near Beaufort, hired Francis Griswold to write what became the next best thing to *Gone With the Wind.* Griswold's *A Sea Island Lady* tells the story of the wealthy antebellum cotton society that in one day truly was gone with the wind, Beaufort, South Carolina. Reaching a popularity just short of its more illustrious predecessor, *A Sea Island Lady* remains the second best novel about the Civil War.

■ **Gullah folklorists and sociologists**. Serious academicians have discovered in the social complex of the Sea Islands rich material for fashioning sociological studies. The folk-culture movement of the early 20th century brought a most wealthy and independent-minded woman, Elsie Clews Parsons, to Beaufort in 1919 to write *Folk-Lore of the Sea Islands*. In this book she preserved hundreds of the Gullah folk tales and riddles handed down from generation to generation in the oral tradition of the black residents on St. Helena Island. In 1930 T.J. Woofter, Jr., compiled his Social Science Research Council study of black culture here into a lyrical book titled *Black Yoemanry, Life on St. Helena Island*, dedicated to Rossa B. Cooley and Grace B. House, the two women who devoted their lives to Penn School after Laura Towne died. Also in 1930 appeared Guion Griffis Johnson's *A Social History of the Sea Islands*, the most brilliant and exhaustive study of traditional black culture on St. Helena Island.

■ **Sea Island historians and photographers**. In 1964 the eminent Johns Hopkins University history professor Willie Lee Rose published her masterpiece, *Rehearsal for Reconstruction, the Port Royal Experiment*, chronicling the efforts of the Federal military and civilian occupation forces to set free, feed, clothe, educate, employ, pay, and auction land to the 10,000 slaves they found here in 1861. Edith M. Dabbs in 1971 brought the images of the islanders to life in *Face of an Island, Leigh Richmond Miner's photographs of Saint Helena Island*. These are photographs taken in the 1890s and 1920s that rival ones by Walker Evans in *Let Us Now Praise Famous Men*, the 1930s' photographic essay that includes famous photographs Evans took here. A compelling 1983 photographic essay is Jack Leigh's *Oystering, A Way of Life*. Ronald Daise followed in 1986 with his *Reminiscences of Sea Island Heritage*, historical photographs from the York Bailey Museum at Penn Community Center. In 1996 Lawrence

Rowland and George Rogers, history professors at the University of South Carolina, issued their monumental work, *The History of Beaufort County, South Carolina: 1514-1861*.

■ **Great American novelist.** When Thomas Wolfe published in 1929 his thinly-veiled autobiography, *Look Homeward, Angel*, about his family and life in Asheville, North Carolina, critics of American literature hailed it as the great American novel of the 20th century. They failed to anticipate Pat Conroy, whose autobiographical novels about his family and life in Beaufort, South Carolina, have become the great American novels of our time. So unknown as to have to pay someone to publish his first book, *The Boo*, Conroy converted his disappointment over being fired from his teaching job by the Beaufort County Board of Education in 1970 into *The Water is Wide*. Next came lyrical descriptions of the Lowcountry and Herculean struggles with his father and the world in *The Great Santini*, *The Prince of Tides*, *The Lords of Discipline*, and *Beach Music*. Through extremely popular motion pictures, Conroy's books have been carried around the world to people who until Conroy had never heard of beautiful Beaufort by the sea.

We would fail in describing the rich literary legacy of Beaufort unless we also included the names of other writers, some of them very famous, who have lived and written here—Mason Locke Weems, W. Somerset Maugham, Samuel Hopkins Adams, Samuel Henry Rogers, Ella Worth Pendergast, Lena Wood Lengnick, Ann Head, Chlotilde Martin, Gary Black, Ed McTeer, George McMillan, Priscilla McMillan, Cecily McMillan, Roy Attaway, Marjorie Montgomery, Fred Trask, Valerie Sayers, Gerhard Spieler, Charlton Ogburn, Ervin Greene, Lois Battle, Gloria Naylor, Carl Smith, Charlotte Hughes, Carl Eby, Roy Flannagan, Sara Harrell Banks, and a host of others.

Winship Durrett

Glorious daffodils announce the beginning of spring in Beaufort in mid February, just in time for St. Valentine's day.

A Beaufort Calendar

■ **Springtime Flowers.** Winters in Beaufort are short and mild, seeming like spring to visitors from colder parts of the country. During camellia season in January the Beaufort Council of Garden Clubs sponsors a flower show. Springtime flowers burst forth in the middle of February, especially notable being the fields of daffodils on Cane Island (see photo opposite). Azaleas bloom in mid-March and continue through mid-April.

■ **Spring Tour of Homes.** St. Helena's Episcopal Church sponsors the spring tour of homes each March. Tours of privately-owned historic homes, gardens, and plantations in the Beaufort area are featured. The tours attract visitors from all over the world, so make reservations for accommodations early.

■ **A Taste of Beaufort.** Sponsored by Mainstreet Beaufort, this food, wine, and arts festival takes place on a Saturday each spring in the downtown waterfront park. You can spend the day and evening viewing art displays and children's crafts, munching on good food from the best local restaurants, sipping good wine and beer from all over the world, listening to great local musical entertainment, and basking in the glory of the waterfront.

■ **Gullah Festival.** The Gullah festival is a celebration of Sea Island heritage, showcasing gospel and jazz music, storytelling, Gullah language exhibits, fine-arts displays, folklore, and crafts. This festival has gained recognition as one of the most important celebrations of African-American culture in the nation. The festival is held on Memorial Day weekend with activities centered around the downtown waterfront park.

■ **Beaufort Water Festival.** Perhaps Beaufort's biggest event of the year, the water festival lasts almost two weeks each July. Among the featured events are boat races, fishing tournaments, aerial shows, dances, concerts, a hometown parade, antique and art shows, a beauty pageant, water ski shows, and more. Bring your boat if you have one; the sandbar in the Beaufort River gets heavily populated for this event.

■ **Festival of Homes and History.** Each October Historic Beaufort Foundation sponsors this tour of privately-owned historic homes, gardens, and plantations in the area. Visitors come from all over the world, so make your arrangements for accommodations far in advance, especially if you wish to stay in the downtown historic district.

Beaufort's historic houses and gardens receive loving care from homeowners in preparation for the annual fall and spring tours.

■ **Beaufort Shrimp Festival.** The shrimp festival takes place on a Saturday in September, October, or November (depends on the shrimp season) on the waterfront in downtown Beaufort. This seafood feast with shrimp dishes prepared by local restaurants includes family games and musical entertainment. Local bubbas dock their shrimp boats along the seawall at the waterfront park.

■ **St. Helena's Bazaar.** The second Saturday in November brings bargain hunters and crafts lovers to St. Helena Episcopal Church's bazaar, a Beaufort tradition for more than 50 years. Handmade items, garden and house plants, old books, clothing, and plenty of tasty food can be purchased at this annual event at the parish house at 507 Newcastle Street. Be sure to arrive early for a choice of the best bargains.

■ **Heritage Festival** is a popular celebration of African-American and Sea Island culture for the benefit of Penn Center. Held on the Penn Center campus on St. Helena Island, the festival takes place over three days and features African-American art exhibitions, a cultural symposium, a fish fry and oyster roast, blues singing, a parade, folk arts, and Lowcountry foods.

■ **Holiday Season.** The holiday season in downtown Beaufort expresses the spirit of Christmas with window-decoration contests, tree-lighting ceremonies, a parade of festooned boats in the Bay at dusk, and a real old-fashioned Christmas parade down Bay Street. A particularly enjoyable event is Night on the Town when the downtown merchants invite everybody into their shops for homemade goodies and Christmas cheer. Bay Street is closed to vehicles so that people can meander freely, entertainment from jazz to madrigals is on every corner, and the evening peaks with the lighting of the town Christmas tree.

George Trask

Beaufort's mild climate makes gardening a favorite outdoor activity every month of the year.

Beaufort Out of Doors

THE GREAT OUT OF DOORS beckons you every month of the year at Beaufort. Weather is, of course, the controlling factor in enjoying outdoor sports and nature activities, and the weather here is almost always favorable. You can divide Beaufort's climate into two major categories, cool and warm. The cool weather lasts eight months, spanning all of autumn, winter, and spring. Warm weather dominates the summer. Hot summer days in Beaufort truly are less burdensome than hot summer days in Washington and New York City, for there is almost always a sea breeze here. In addition to swimming and sunning at the magnificent oceanfront beach at Hunting Island, outdoor activities entice you throughout the year—golf, tennis, hunting, fishing, boating, sailing, gardening, nature watching, you name it.

Oceanfront Beach

One of the finest and most popular state parks on the entire Atlantic coast is Hunting Island, located just 20 minutes by car from downtown Beaufort. Miles of wide sandy beach await you. The surf, the seashells, the bird life, the old lighthouse, and the towering overstory of live oak and palmetto trees make Hunting Island State Park worth a visit by everyone. Parents with young children will especially welcome the gentle surf. There are campgrounds, nature trails, a boardwalk through the marsh, and many other enticements. From the beach you can see shrimp boats trawling the ocean, followed by gulls and pelicans. Summertime is, or course, the best time to take a swim, but Hunting Island will attract you at all times throughout the year, when a stroll on the beach can bring peace and quiet.

Golf Courses

Some of the most famous and challenging golf courses in the world are located on Hilton Head Island in Beaufort county. There are also the following outstanding courses just minutes from Beaufort's downtown historic district:

■ **Country Club of Beaufort at Pleasant Point**, 18 holes, designed by Russell Breedon, located at Pleasant Point Plantation on Lady's Island.

■ **Country Club of Callawassie**, 27 holes, designed by Tom Fazio, located on Callawassie Island, just across the Broad River bridge.

■ **Dataw Island Golf Course**, 36 holes, available only to residents and prospective residents of Dataw Island.

■ **Fripp Island Ocean Point Golf Links**, 18 holes, on the ocean at Fripp Island. To play at Fripp, you must set up an appointment or you will not be allowed through the gate.

■ **Golf Professionals Club**, 36 holes, on Sam's Point Road, Lady's Island. Guest play is welcome on either the Champions or the Players Course.

■ **South Carolina National Golf Club**, 18 holes, on Cat Island, designed by George W. Cobb. A fully stocked pro shop and club rentals are available, also a grill and lounge.

■ **Tabby Links at Spring Island**, 18-holes, designed by Arnold Palmer and Ed Seay. Considered by many to be the finest course of Palmer's career, this course is restricted to members and their guests.

Boating and Sailing

One of the best ways to see the beauty of Beaufort is from the water, which literally provided the only access to the town and the neighboring islands before the bridges were built. With the rivers and creeks defining our way of life, it would be a shame to miss this part of the Beaufort experience. A thrilling scene is the approach to downtown Beaufort on the river from the south. Sunsets are an especially gorgeous time of the day. There are many boat tours to choose from, information available at the downtown marina. Be sure to double check departure times and weather conditions. And don't forget your sunscreen.

Our wide, protected bays are perfect places for sailboating, and regattas are held here in summertime. Because Beaufort is on the Intracoastal Waterway, the town is host to sailors and boat travelers from all over the world. For those who are not familiar, the Intracoastal Waterway is a network of inlets, rivers, creeks, and waterways along the Atlantic and Gulf coasts. They connect to form a water highway by which one may travel by boat all the way from New England to Texas without going out into the ocean. This waterway is especially pleasurable because of its numerous delightful ports and the protection afforded by river inlets.

The downtown marina, located at the city's downtown waterfront park, offers overnight dockage with electricity, water, fuel, showers, laundry facilities, and a marina store. You can walk to all the downtown restaurants and shops as well as get a restful night's sleep at Best Western Sea Island Inn and Port Republic Inn, located just across the street from the marina.

Another nearby place to dock your boat is Port Royal Landing Marina, located near the McTeer bridge on the Beaufort River. It has overnight dockage with electricity, water, fuel, showers, laundry facilities, and a marina store. There is an on-site bar and restaurant with good food and drink and a great chicken salad sandwich. There is plenty of deep water and the approach is easy, but be ready for fast currents.

Public ramps abound in our county where you may launch your trailer-borne boat. For example, there is a small ramp downtown at the end of the seawall by the downtown marina, a larger one immediately across the bridge on Lady's Island, and an even larger one at the Broad River bridge.

If you are new to our waters, we urge you to consult tide and nautical charts and waterway guides before exploring. Our tides are extreme, shoals are everywhere, and the currents are treacherous at times. If you are not careful you can end up with your boat stranded on an invisible muddy bottom. Worse, you and your boat can be swept out into the ocean by the fast moving tides. An ounce of prevention is worth a pound of cure.

Beaufort boys engage in one of their favorite summertime activities, circa 1959.

Fishing

The creeks, rivers, and ocean surrounding the Beaufort area are renowned for onshore and offshore fishing. Shrimp, crabs, oysters, clams, and flounders are free for the taking in the creeks. Numerous game fish abound in the rivers and the ocean including sea trout, redfish, cobia, tarpon, blue fish, and king mackerel.

Many fishing opportunities are available to satisfy both serious and whimsical fishermen. The quickest and perhaps the easiest is to drop a line off the seawall at the downtown waterfront park. The sides of numerous bridges also provide quick access to fishing holes. The Broad River bridge has an excellent fishing pier. Paradise Pier is another favorite of local anglers, located at the southern tip of Hunting Island.

George Trask

Fishing "captains" after a day at the wreck off Hunting Island, a favorite fishing hole.

Downtown Bay Street displays the town clock, a reminder of a simpler time, at the entrance to the downtown waterfront park.

Beaufort's Local Color

Interesting small towns have the reputation of being places filled beyond their sizes with colorful people and colorful stories. Every place, of course, has a story to tell. Large cities have so many stories that they tend to be swallowed in the rush of crowds and events. Only in small towns does time run slow enough to allow savoring the special highlights that touch everyone. Here are several of the local colors that make up Beaufort's rainbow of moments and memories:

■ **Fordham Hardware** has been a fixture at the corner of Bay and Carteret Streets since 1946. Need a hammock? Some wood glue? Zucchini seed? Fordham has offered everything imaginable that a hardware merchant should sell, from nails by

George Trask

the ounce to fertilizer and wheelbarrows. Generations of Beaufortonians have known the members of the Fordham family who have kept this downtown icon of old Beaufort alive so many years—six siblings, Angus, Bart, Mae, Pete, Mark, and Saise Fordham, and now Angus's son, Duncan Fordham. Every town should be so fortunate as to have a Fordham Hardware.

■ **Lipsitz Department Store** on Bay Street. Imagine Beaufort in 1902: dirt streets, horse-drawn carriages, and Lipsitz Department Store. Still going strong a century later, Lipsitz is famous for shoes: Stride Rite, Top Sider, Keds, Rockport, and Naturalizers. They are also headquarters for Oshkosh, Levi's, and other good old American clothes brands. The most famous of all downtown dwellers, "Lippy" the mynah bird, resided here, charming natives and visitors with endless chatter, until replaced by a mute mynah bird. Joseph Lipsitz, son of Max Lipsitz, the founder, celebrated his 80th birthday in Y2K, still welcoming his customers in the original store. His son, Neil, built a new shoe emporium across the street, making clear the family's determination to carry the Lipsitz retailing name for another 100 years on Bay Street.

■ **Old Jericho Road**. Writings about Beaufort before automobiles destroyed pastoral beauty almost always began with a description of tree-covered roads leading to town. Portions of one, Old Jericho Road, still exist, a winding lane paralleling S.C. Highway 280 between Burton and Shell Point. Walking or driving down Old Jericho Road with its ancient oaks and quiet fields transports one back in time to the days when the ox-cart was the principal mode of transportation here.

Beaufort Overnight

OWNTOWN BEAUFORT IS BLESSED with outstanding hostelries. You'll want to consider staying downtown because within walking distance will be historic houses, specialty shopping, outstanding restaurants, the waterfront park, everything that makes the historic district of old Beaufort unique. Good accommodations are also available at inns affiliated with national chains, located on the highways leading into town. Here are some of our favorite places to stay.

■ **Beaufort Inn**, 809 Port Republic Street, is an elegant bed & breakfast with an outstanding restaurant serving some of the best food and wine in this part of the country. Julia Roberts stayed here during the filming of *Something to Talk About*.

■ **Cuthbert House Inn**, 1203 Bay Street, is located on the waterfront in the historic Bay Street residential neighborhood. If you're a Civil War buff you'll especially enjoy spending the night in the same house General William Tecumseh Sherman visited just before his army invaded South Carolina.

■ **Port Republic Inn**, 915 Port Republic Street, occupies a gracious antebellum structure built in 1820. Perfectly located in the downtown historic district, it features spacious suites lavishly restored and furnished with period antiques. Each suite has its own living room, fireplace, bedroom, bathroom, and kitchen. A perfect combination of high quality and bargain price.

■ **Rhett House Inn**, 1009 Craven Street, is a renowned, expensive bed & breakfast that has grown to include an annex across the street. The original part of the inn is located in the historic Thomas Moore Rhett house, built c. 1820.

■ **Best Western Sea Island Inn**, 1015 Bay Street, is complete with meeting and banquet rooms and a private pool in a secluded courtyard. Its 43 rooms offer every comfort. The location on the waterfront site of the historic Sea Island Hotel has made it the most popular place to stay in downtown Beaufort for generations. Saturday night dances were held in the ballroom of the old hotel, razed in 1960, and a bathhouse and pavilion were located across the street on the waterfront, now the location of the downtown marina. Historic homes, downtown shops, restaurants, and the waterfront park are just a few steps away.

Sea Island Hotel was razed in 1960 to make way for the Sea Island Inn, located on the Bay overlooking the waterfront park.

New to Beaufort

MANY VISITORS WHO come to Beaufort are so enamored of the town that they decide to retire or have a second home in the area. You can fulfill your dream here, overlooking the ocean, the waterway, the vast expanses of marshland, a golf course, or woodlands of pines and live oaks. In addition to the historic neighborhoods in town, the following planned communities are considered to be especially attractive places to live.

■ **Brays Island**, with 5000 acres of woodlands, pastures, ponds, and marshes, is a sportsman's paradise. This exclusive, low-density community definitely appeals to the upper crust.

■ **Callawassie Island** is a golfing paradise about 15 miles southwest of Beaufort. Tom Fazio designed the 27-hole golf course which takes up most of the recreational time of the residents. Golf fairways as well as homesites overlook the surrounding marshes.

■ **Cane Island** is a small, quiet island about three miles from downtown Beaufort. The homesites are spacious with choices overlooking the Beaufort River and a large fresh water pond. No golfers or beachgoers here, just abundant, peaceful, undisturbed nature.

■ **Cat Island**. This island is on the Beaufort River just past Cane Island. A George Cobb golf course is in the center of the island with homes and homesites along the waterfront, marsh, and golf course.

■ **Dataw Island** is a community of upscale homes and well-manicured lawns. A favorite of corporate retirees, Dataw has two golf courses (one designed by Tom Fazio), a marina, a large club house with an excellent restaurant, and miles of nature trails for biking and hiking.

■ **Distant Island.** Our favorite waterfront community is a paradise, covered with live oaks and other mature trees, and located just a few minutes by car from downtown Beaufort. Distant Island views the Intracoastal Waterway and Port Royal Sound, which can be reached in minutes by boats of all sizes.

■ **Fripp Island.** It is almost impossible to stay indoors on a sunny day at Fripp. Beachcombers search for shells and sand dollars. Golfers play on the challenging seaside course. Naturalists scan the marshes for birds, deer, small animals, and plant life.

■ **Habersham Plantation.** Located along the Broad River, Habersham is an exquisite blend of neighborhood living and waterfront amenities. Its traditional Lowcountry architecture is just the right prescription for the growth of Beaufort.

■ **Newpoint**, across the river from Beaufort's historic district, is patterned after streets in old Beaufort. Residents can walk along the oak-lined sidewalks to visit with their neighbors or watch the sunset from the waterfront park and community dock.

■ **Spring Island** will delight nature lovers and people who dream of owning an estate on an island. Quail hunting is a Spring Island tradition. Estate-sized homesites overlook the marsh, the river, and golf course designed by Arnold Palmer.

Near to Beaufort

DVENTUROUS VISITORS TO BEAUFORT can spend many happy hours exploring the surrounding towns, none of which is more than about an hour's drive away. Located midway between Charleston and Savannah, Beaufort is the perfect overnight base for day trips to those cities, as well as to nearby Hilton Head Island and Bluffton. Everything from historic homes with lush flower gardens to air-conditioned shopping malls awaits you.

Charleston

Charleston is a pleasant 60-mile drive north of Beaufort along U.S. 17, a route that follows the old colonial trail on the mainland through rice fields and cypress swamps and across pristine rivers. This city, dating back to its establishment in 1670, has seen it all: bellicose Indians, frightful hurricanes, destructive earthquakes, tragic yellow fever, ruinous boll weevils, and two major wars on its soil. Major attractions in Charleston include Fort Sumter, where the Civil War started; the Battery, where massive mansions overlook the harbor; and Magnolia Gardens with its winding paths, courtyards, finely manicured open spaces, and lavish green carpets framed by bursting azaleas, camellias, and gardenias.

March and April feature the annual Festival of Houses. From mid-May through June the Spoleto Festival and Piccolo Spoleto, Charleston's most popular and well attended festivals, showcase everything from opera to dramatic arts, chamber music, jazz, ballet, art exhibits, and poetry readings. October features the Moja Arts Festival. While many of these events charge admission, there are still many free events for the day tripper, such as The Citadel corps of cadets dress parade, concerts at

Hampton Park, and College of Charleston's recital series on Monday evenings.

The Charleston Museum, founded in 1773, is the oldest museum in the United States. The Gibbes Art Museum houses portraits, paintings, sketches, and art of all kinds dating back to the 1700s. Also in Charleston is the Avery Research Center for African-American History and Culture, which highlights Gullah art and history. Don't miss the American Military Museum, a tribute to America's military heroes, with artifacts from every branch of the armed services. These museums are all within a brisk walk or a short drive of each other.

The Nathaniel Russell House, circa 1809 and open to the public, is a striking Adam-style house with an unsupported spiral staircase. The College of Charleston, one of America's first city colleges, is in the middle of town and was built in 1828 with money donated by the people of Charleston. Drayton Hall, located out of town on the Ashley River, is a splendid Palladian-style architectural masterpiece now owned by the National Trust for Historic Preservation and open to the public.

Shopping along King and Bay Streets is a charming walk through cobblestone streets. The old market district is a nice stroll where you will find sweetgrass baskets (made in front of you by the women who sell them), used books, homemade jams and jellies, and handmade quilts—everything distinctly Southern and lovelier than the average souvenir fare offered in most city shopping districts. At every turn in the downtown area are ancient churches, public parks, specialty shops, outstanding restaurants, hotels and inns, and major stores including Saks Fifth Avenue.

Savannah

Georgia's bustling seaport city of Savannah, site of the novel *In the Garden of Good and Evil*, is located less than an hour's drive south of Beaufort. From its modest beginnings as a colony of 144 Englishmen in 1735, to its later position as one of the commercial centers of the antebellum South, to its present-day status as a busy seaport and tourist destination, Savannah has been an important city throughout the history of America.

Visitors can admire monuments, greenery, and flowers in Savannah's 24 town squares, which were all part of General James E. Oglethorpe's original plan for the city. Savannah also has the largest historic district of any city in the United States. Over 1,500 historically significant structures have survived two devastating fires, neither of which was set by General W.T. Sherman, who arrived here in late 1864 after his famous Civil War march from Atlanta to the sea.

In fact, Savannah so impressed General Sherman that he "gave" the city to President Lincoln as a Christmas present in 1864. It is beyond the scope of this book to present an account of Savannah's rich history and points of interest, but suffice it to say that a trip to this extraordinary city would be a high point of any visit to the Lowcountry.

From Beaufort, take Highway 170 all the way to Savannah's historic district, located just over the high bridge across the Savannah River. Off Oglethorpe Avenue you will encounter Savannah's stately historic district, with landscaped squares and antebellum homes galore. Bay Street and River Street are where you will find restaurants, taverns, and specialty shops. There are tours of all kinds available whether you want to walk, ride in a horse-drawn carriage, or board one of Savannah's many riverboats. The Savannah Convention and Visitor's Bureau can give you the lowdown on everything you will want to know about this historic city.

Hilton Head Island

There was no permanent settlement on Hilton Head Island until about 1717, when several families acquired large tracts of land and began farming operations. After the American Revolution, cotton made these plantation owners wealthy. The Federal invasion in November 1861 brought nearly 15,000 Union soldiers to occupy the island throughout the Civil War. Labor brigades built military buildings and made improvements to Fort Walker, renamed Fort Welles by the Unionists.

Poverty followed the war. Wealthy northerners bought the large tracts of land here in the early decades of the 20th century to use for hunting and sporting retreats. In the early 1950s, Charles Fraser envisioned a community on the island where people could enjoy nature's beauty alongside their favorite outdoor pastimes, without destroying the natural environment. He routed roads around oak trees and built houses the color of natural surroundings with natural vegetation intact. He installed board walkways across sand dunes to the beach, siting houses behind the dunes instead of bulldozing them. He built bicycle paths through the woods and set aside hundreds of acres as nature preserves. He outlawed garish commercial signage and monitored architecture to keep the visual impact of homes and businesses to a minimum.

The result is Sea Pines, the model for all subsequent communities on Hilton Head Island and a prototype for environmentally friendly communities everywhere. The island now hosts nearly a million visitors each year to its golf courses, tennis courts, ocean beaches, wildlife, and shopping. The Heritage Golf Classic and the Family Circle Tennis Cup draw sports enthusiasts the world over. The Hilton Head Art League, Hilton Head Orchestra, Hilton Head Jazz Society, and Hilton Head Playhouse provide opportunities to enjoy art, music, and theater. All of this, and miles of white, sandy beaches, too.

Bluffton

Bluffton is the formerly little town on the mainland just before the bridge to Hilton Head Island. It has suddenly become a huge town through annexation of vast tracts of timberland, formerly owned by Union Camp Corporation, now slated for upscale residential development.

Bluffton was created as a summer refuge for wealthy antebellum families, and named for the high bluffs upon which they built their houses. The movement for South Carolina's secession from the Union had its roots in Bluffton. Summer resident Robert Barnwell Rhett began his long battle with the U.S. government over the "Tariff of Abominations," which reduced cotton exports to England for the benefit of Northern manufacturers. He was a leading proponent of the "Bluffton Movement for a State Convention," and eventually helped to draft the Ordinance of Secession in his home town of Beaufort.

A small number of Confederates, who had grown up in the area and were angry at the Union occupation of their family lands, were stationed at Bluffton during the Civil War. Their nighttime raids on Union-occupied Hilton Head Island so infuriated the Federal officers that they sent three vessels of troops to destroy Bluffton in 1863. When the Southern plantation families returned after the war, they found almost all of their homes in ruins.

In the past two years Bluffton has become like Hilton Head, mushrooming in automobile traffic, retail activity, new construction, and size. The Del Webb retirement community known as Sun City Hilton Head is currently being built near Bluffton, and more retirement-communities are being announced every day. Old-time Blufftonians are holding their breaths to see if their town can retain its character in the face of this onslaught.

Daufuskie Island

Daufuskie Island lies across Calibogue Sound, southwest of Hilton Head Island. Accessible only by boat, it remains a backwater of the Sea Islands but is emerging in fits and starts into the modern world.

Daufuskie's history mirrored that of Hilton Head until the 1950s, when Hilton Head began its ascent as one of the world's premier resort islands. Unlike Hilton Head, Daufuskie still remains a quiet place, populated primarily by descendants of the African slaves who once worked the cotton plantations there. The Gullah dialect spoken by Daufuskie residents can still be heard today. The traditional occupations of the islanders are fishing, farming, and oystering. Pat Conroy's best-selling novel, *The Water is Wide*, tells of his experiences as a secondary school teacher on Daufuskie in 1970 and of his sometimes frustrating interactions with young Daufuskie students and the Beaufort county educational authorities.

In the 1980s, the resorts of Melrose and Haig Point brought the outside world to Daufuskie. Still a far cry from fast-paced Hilton Head, these areas are juxtaposed against the rural backdrop of the traditional culture. A trip around the non-resort areas of Daufuskie will show the visitor that the traditional residents still enjoy the tranquil lifestyle of this isolated, rural Sea Island where nothing much has ever happened.

Afterword

WELL, AS YOU CAN TELL, beautiful Beaufort by the sea and its nearby areas have a lot to offer. Some might think of Beaufort as a return to the past. Not so. Beaufort is very much a part of the modern world with the area having one of the youngest, fastest growing, and most prosperous populations in the state.

Beaufort is a wonderful place to live. The people here are committed to making sure Beaufort will remain that way. This means being generous with praise for the values that make Beaufort special and skeptical of proposals that might threaten its uniqueness.

We like to think of Beaufort as a precursor of the future, an expression of the way people are supposed to live—in harmony with each other and with nature. So when you come here, either as visitor or settler, please remember to say a good word and smile. And do a good deed. In Beaufort, these characteristics are contagious.

Frogmore, S.C., May 14, 1871

I do never intend to leave. I intend to end my days here and I wish to.

—*Letters and Diary of Laura M. Towne, written from the Sea Islands of South Carolina, 1862-1884*, edited by Rupert Sargent Holland, 1912

Index